BLUEPRINT

HOMESCHOOLING

How to Plan a Year of Home Education

That Fits the Reality of Your Life

AMY KNEPPER

Park Day Publishing

Ventura, California

BLUEPRINT HOMESCHOOLING

Published by Park Day Publishing

Ventura, CA

First print edition: November 2014

ISBN-13: 978-0-9862249-0-4
ISBN-10: 0986224901

www.blueprinthomeschooling.com

For Sarah, Angela, and Janessa, because they asked.

Part Four: Curriculum

Part Five: Calendars

Part Six: Making It Work

Part Seven: Final Notes

Contents

Introduction to *Blueprint Homeschooling*

This book isn't really about planning. After you've gone through it, you'll have a great plan for your school year, but that's just a bonus. This book is really about dreaming, envisioning, discovering, and preparing an ideal year of homeschooling for your whole family. Rather than having you fill in a bunch of charts and calendars, I will walk you through the process of discovering why you homeschool, what you hope each of your children will get out of homeschooling, and how you will make those dreams happen with a solid, workable plan.

By the time you're done reading this book and working through some of the questions and projects included in each section, you'll have two plans, or blueprints, for your year. Your first blueprint will be the one for your dream home: your ideal homeschool year. If you had unlimited time, energy, money, and resources, this is the plan you would go with. Your second blueprint will be the one for the house you live in while you build your dream home. This is the homeschool year that is interrupted by illnesses, unplanned activities, unexpected visitors, and those days when no one, including you, wants to do anything.

I think it is rare for two families to have the same dream for their homeschool year. Just as people live in all sorts of different houses, they will value different things in the education of their children. One homeschool year might be like living in an igloo: streamlined and simple and short on amenities. Another family's homeschool year might be like Disneyland: full of costume parties, beautiful images, and sensational experiences. Your ideal year will probably fall somewhere in between those two extremes.

I have been homeschooling my two children for six years now. When I first started, I felt like I was wandering down a dark hallway, looking for a light switch. What do I teach? What do I need to prepare? What supplies do I need? Am I doing this right? Am I really qualified for this? What if I miss something important?

The planning process in this book is the way I answer all those questions. I have been planning this way for four years. Every year is a little different from the last, but each time I go through this process I get a clearer view of the work ahead and more confidence that I can complete it. As you go through the process, you'll find your values, set your goals, and then choose some very concrete ways of managing your expectations through the school year. You'll also learn some tricks to keep encouragement visible so that you don't fall prey to winter despair and give up. I hope this process will help you as much as it has helped me.

Frequently Asked Questions

Who is this book for?

Blueprint Homeschooling is for anyone looking for a better way to plan a homeschool year. Maybe you're brand new to homeschooling and you're looking for help getting started. I hope this book encourages you and offers ideas about how to make it work for you and your family.

Maybe you're a veteran homeschooler with a few wild years already under your belt. Maybe you feel like you're missing something or it seems like things are too hectic. Maybe you're like me and need a little encouragement and some fresh ideas to liven things up a bit. I hope you find something here to help you keep going.

Maybe you aren't a homeschooler yet, but you're considering your educational options. In that case, I hope this book helps you better visualize what homeschooling might look like for your family.

How do I use this book?

Blueprint Homeschooling contains a variety of tasks and exercises you can do to help you plan a full year of homeschooling activities in advance. I recommend you read through it twice—once to get an overview of the process, and a second time in order to answer the questions and do the project suggestions that you find helpful.

I've arranged this book to take a top-down approach to planning. At the beginning, we'll be exploring values and answering the big question: "Why?" We're going to talk about the things that are most important to you as a person, as an educator, and as a homeschooling family. Please don't skip this step. I think it's the most important part of the whole process. Find your big picture first, and all those little details will fall into place.

After exploring values, we'll talk about the different methods you might use that would fit your values for education. I'll offer some different ideas to help you find the curriculum or methods that would be of most value for you. While you read, I want you to keep an open mind about your family and your methods. You've probably been told a lot of things about what you should do and how you should go about this thing called homeschooling. Forget all that for a little bit and use this process to imagine the best possible methods for you and your family.

After that, we'll talk about goal setting. This is where you'll dream up some possibilities for long-term goals and then whittle them down to things you can do this year, this month, or even this week. Then, and only then, we'll get to calendars and charts and all the nuts and bolts that keep things going during the year. I'll show you how to look ahead through your year to block out time for recurring events and holidays. I'll show you how to educate in the midst of your busiest seasons. We'll break everything down by months, weeks, and days so you can see exactly how much time and effort you and your children will be putting in to meet your goals. We'll adjust those schedules to make them more realistic, dropping or adding things as needed.

Then we'll make another set of goals—the bare minimums you need to complete should anything happen to disrupt your year. This is the plan you'll go to for extended illnesses, a move, a new baby, or any unexpected issue that might make homeschooling difficult.

By the time you're done, you'll have a workable plan, a shopping list for all the supplies you might need, and clear goals for what you'll accomplish. You'll also have a values statement to keep you focused on the things that are most important to you.

What if I'm not an organized person?

Many of my friends like to tell me how disorganized they are.

These are the same friends who have more than three kids and multiple pets, who manage long family camping trips in the wilderness, or who decorate their houses based on a different time period every few months. These same friends go crazy for holidays, giving small handmade presents to everyone they've ever known. Every time they tell me they're disorganized, I have to laugh in disbelief.

Give yourself some credit. If you're considering homeschooling, it means you most likely have at least one child who is nearing school age. From that, I can assume you've managed some sort of meal planning, grocery shopping, and child care. You've probably made it to at least half a dozen doctor appointments (more if you have a daredevil for a child). You've probably done more holiday and event planning than you ever wanted to do, because there are birthday parties and holidays and family events that happen almost constantly throughout a year. You probably have other hobbies and interests. Maybe you like reading books on homeschool planning or education. If so, you are more organized than you think.

If you don't feel organized, then I hope this book will help you better understand how to do things in your own style, in a way that already works in your life. Rather than give you a bunch of charts and spreadsheets that you don't know how to use, I'm going to help you figure out what tools would work for you and then show you how and why to use them.

How do I find the time?

This is by far the most common question people ask me when I mention this planning process. Homeschool parents usually feel like they are spread thin. Often, they are operating on one income, with a stay-at-home parent that is constantly taking on time-sensitive child care tasks. How in the world can you spend time doing all this planning work? My answer to the time question is this:

You'll spend the time somewhere.

You'll spend the time searching for supplies when your kids want to do an experiment. You'll spend the time looking for books to read at the library, when all the books you really want are checked out by someone else. You'll spend time and money purchasing curricula at full price that will end up sitting on your shelves unused. You'll spend the time during the summer, trying to help your kids finish up that math curriculum or that writing curriculum you committed to. Or you'll spend the time worrying in the middle of the night whether you're doing the right thing or whether you're missing something.

Invest a little time in this process before you start your school year, and you may find that it gives you more time when you need it.

I block out a week or two during the summer when I don't have other obligations. If your kids go to camp, or they spend a week at Vacation Bible School or some other similar event, take that time to get your planning done. Or if you're spending a day at the beach or the park, take your planning things with you. It's really not too hard once you get started.

Why should I plan an entire year in advance?

I get this question quite often, too. How can you plan for an entire year when you don't even know what you're making for dinner tonight? It seems too far-fetched to try to plan for something that's not going to happen for another eight months.

Sure, no one really knows what's going to happen in a year. But there are a lot of things we can expect to happen, because they happen each and every year. During the last several years, these things have happened every year in my family:

Fall

Halloween

Thanksgiving

Family birthdays

Christmas

New Year's

Winter

Flu Season

Valentine's Day

St. Patrick's Day

Easter

Spring

More family birthdays

Gardening Season

Ballet recitals

Chess Tournaments

Local Festivals

There are always a lot of end-of-the-school-year events that happen during May and June as well. We usually have many different occasions to attend like recitals, performances, competitions, fairs, tournaments, parties, and graduations.

If your family participates in sports, you can mark your calendar by the sports seasons: football, soccer, basketball, baseball, gymnastics, hockey, volleyball, or swimming. What sports do you participate in? Whether you plan for them or not, these seasons are going to happen just like they do every year. If you're not expecting them, it's easy to get overwhelmed or feel overloaded during the holidays and tournament seasons.

Instead of letting your calendar control you year after year, why not take a little time to control your calendar? You might find that this year will go much smoother with just a little bit of preparation.

When should I do this?

If this process is going to take some time, when should you do it? There are a few periods of time that work better for me, but you should do it whenever the time is right for you.

I do the bulk of my planning during the two weeks right after a school year ends. There are a few reasons I've started doing it this way.

First, the year we just finished is fresh in my mind. I can think of all the things we forgot or didn't get to. I know where the kids are in things like math, reading, and writing skills. And I'm usually worn out, which makes it easier to set realistic goals rather than overly optimistic ones.

One of the most important reasons I plan in mid-June is the sales. At the end of the school year, teachers have garage sales, homeschoolers get rid of their used curricula, and school supply catalogs often offer hefty discounts. School supplies might not go on sale until July or August, but in the meantime, I can get all the books and curricula I need at garage sales and used curriculum sales.

By planning in early June, I can spend the prime sales months purchasing what I need at a discount, and I have plenty of time before the next year starts to shop for the best prices.

I haven't always done it this way. Sometimes I plan in the fall, just before a school year starts. If you're the type to reminisce and set new goals for the New Year, you might enjoy planning your homeschool year during your holiday breaks. If you school year-round, you can go through this process during one of your longer breaks or whenever you feel like you need a fresh outlook on your schooling.

What if you're in the middle of a school year and you feel swamped by it? Take a week off, go through this process, and see if it doesn't help you clarify the rest of your year. Whenever and where ever you are, you can start.

Once you've started the process, try to finish it within two weeks. I recommend this because all the pieces will be fresh in your mind as you move through the process. If you try to do it in chunks, you might forget what you've done before, and your plans will seem disjointed.

Try to do it all in one shorter time period, and I think you'll find you have more cohesive plans. Plus, it won't be weighing on your mind.

Are you ready? Let's get started!

Part One: Values

Building without plans

When my son was three or four years old, I started thinking about preschool options. At that time, I wasn't sure if I was going to homeschool or not, so preschool was my trial run. I set up bulletin boards and colorful calendars and started teaching letters and animals and colors. As he got older, I shifted into phonics, pre-kindergarten workbooks, and math flash cards. When he was five and officially not going to a public kindergarten, I became his full-time teacher and took it upon myself to do everything I could to make it *feel* like kindergarten.

Now I watch other young parents go through the same cycle, and I have to wonder why. Why do we do all these things in exactly this way, without really thinking through it all? I know that in my case, I felt like I needed to prove myself. I had to prove that I could educate my own children. So I took it upon myself to do more than they do in schools. I did more crafts, more glitter, more books, and more work. Now I look back and wonder how many of those activities are the equivalent of setting up a plum stand in the back yard. All of it looks good and I worked really hard, but was it the best thing to do at the time?

I think many of us go into this homeschooling thing without really knowing what we want. It's as though someone just gave me an acre of land and I decide to build a house on it. I've seen houses before. I've been in other people's houses. So I put together some twigs and branches and try to build my own house. But it won't stay up. It's not keeping the rain out. Why isn't it the dream house I was hoping for?

Before you build a house, you need plans. You need blueprints.

Today, we're going to take a step back from all the fuss about socialization and standardization and doing things the way they've always been done, and we're going to put together a set of blueprints for your homeschool year. The first thing we're going to talk about will help you build the foundation of your house. We're going to talk about why you homeschool and what that looks like for your family. We're going to take a good long look at values.

What are values?

Let's imagine for a moment that you have all the time, money, and resources you need to build a new home. Going back to the idea of creating a blueprint, the first thing we need to know is, "Where in the world are we going to build this thing?" Depending on the location of the home, you'll know what things it has to have.

My parents live in Hawaii. It's always warm there. Until a few months ago, I lived in Washington State, where it's often chilly and rainy. In Washington, we had two major things in our home that my parents in Hawaii do not: a heater and storm windows. My parents wear shorts, light T-shirts, and sandals almost every day. We wore rain jackets, layers of long-sleeved shirts, and shoes that entirely covered our feet. My parents spend their free time at the beach. We spent our free time walking in the local forests. They have to pay attention to tsunami warnings due to earthquakes halfway around the world. We had to pay attention to local river levels because we lived in a flood zone. Now I live in Southern California, where shorts and sandals are an every day occurrence, but rain is not. We still have our differences.

Even though my parents are my family, and even though I look like them and share several mannerisms and traits with them, we live very different lives because we live in such different places.

Homeschoolers, too, can share the same passions but be entirely different from other homeschool families. Why? We have different values.

What are values? To put it simply, values are the ideas or concepts that have the most worth to you. Values are the ideas that drive you. Values tell you where in the world you're building your life. If you value luxury, you will spend your time and money on things you consider luxurious. If you value knowledge, you'll spend your time and money acquiring knowledge—buying books, attending classes, reading, and researching new ideas. If you value family, you'll spend time with your family and participate in family-friendly activities.

One of the easiest ways to discover your values is to put them in terms of dollars. If someone offered you $100 to give up some aspect of your life for one week, what could you give up? What couldn't you give up? Could you give up chocolate? Could you give up access to the Internet? Could you give up using your car? Could you give up your ability to walk? Could you give up your smartphone, your music, or your movies? Some of these things might be easy for you to give up for $100, but others would be difficult or just not worth it.

What about if the offer was raised to $1,000 a week? What could you give up then? I'm not a fan of chocolate, to be honest. I can take it or leave it. But I love my Internet. I can always find answers for things I'm curious about, and can communicate with my friends. Even for $1,000, I'd be hard-pressed to give up the convenience of having answers and entertainment at the click of a mouse.

It might be different for you. You might think Internet connectivity is overrated, but you couldn't imagine giving up a week's worth of coffee, even for $1,000.

Those things you don't want to give up, even for a hefty price, are the things that you value. All of us have values that drive our decisions, but we don't always know what they are. In this chapter, I'm going to focus on helping you discover what your values are as a home educator. Your life and family values might coincide with your values as a homeschooler, but they might not. For this chapter, try to think specifically about home education as you answer the questions and do the exercises.

List your reasons

Some of you may have read the last section and immediately identified your values. "I value literacy above all else!" Others may have looked at all that and thought, "Huh? Give up my coffee? I don't get it." Let's do a few exercises to help you narrow down your values with regards to homeschooling. We'll start by finding out why you homeschool, and then work from there.

A note on supplies: This book contains a series of exercises I call Blueprint Sketches. Many of them will require you to write something down. A lot of it is initial planning: brainstorming and idea generation that happens before we put anything on a calendar. What you use for these exercises is up to you. I use cheap steno pads or notebooks and keep all of my notes and lists in one notebook for each year. It's not pretty, but it works for me. If you want to use pretty planner paper, you'll want something that has a lot of space for notes and lists, especially for the first few sections. You can use scratch paper for the initial planning work, and then a nice planner to put your final plans in. Printer paper works fine. Loose-leaf notebook paper works fine. Sticky notes work fine, but might be a little small for our purposes. Construction paper with crayons will be fine. Use what works for you.

If you are the type to do everything on your computer and back it up in the cloud, that works too. I use Google Drive to store my weekly subject plans, once I've deciphered my almost-legible scribbles from my notebook. If you want to do the entire process on your computer, just create a new folder and keep your new documents inside it. Easy.

This process does not need to look pretty. You don't have to show your friends. No one will check your work later. If it helps you to use your favorite pens and different colors of paper, then do that, but don't feel obligated to make it attractive. You can be as messy and disorganized as you want as you do these exercises. Just try to keep the papers in one place, for your own sanity.

Blueprint Sketch #1: Write to a friend.

> Get out a piece of paper or open a new document on your computer. Pretend that a good friend of yours or a beloved family member is considering homeschooling. They just asked you why you homeschool rather than having your kids in a public or private school. For the sake of this exercise, pretend this person has the same beliefs, the same worldview, and the same lifestyle as you do. They won't be offended by anything you say and won't think you're weird for saying it. If you can't think of a friend or family member, just pretend you're writing to your younger self. Now, spend fifteen minutes writing a letter to convince them they should homeschool. What are the benefits? Why do you choose to do it? Every reason counts. Go.

Blueprint Sketch #2: Enlist the help of your family.

> Let's take that first exercise a step further, shall we? Now, you're going to answer the same question, but this time you'll answer it with the assistance of your family. Gather everyone, get a few sheets of paper, and get ready to write. Ask: "What are some reasons for homeschooling?" Write down all the answers, even the silly ones. Even very young children might have some insightful ideas to offer. When we did this with our family, we had answers as silly as "every day is a pajama day" and as serious as "we get to spend time together instead of being separated all the time." Write them all down.

By the end of these two exercises, you'll probably have a long list of reasons for homeschooling. If you need more ideas, here's a list of reasons for homeschooling compiled from my own lists and from discussions with other homeschoolers online and in person. You may not agree with some of them, but that's okay. See if any of the following are reasons that you choose to homeschool:

~ You like to be home with your kids.

~ One or more of your children has special needs like autism or a learning disorder, or a chronic health issue like diabetes or an auto-immune disorder.

~ You are a (fill in your belief system here) and you don't like the way public schools teach about differing beliefs.

~ Your child has a special goal or skill and needs practice time to master it. Many Olympic athletes are homeschooled or taught by a specialized group of tutors for this reason.

~ You have a degree in education and spent time teaching in public or private schools and decided that you would rather teach your kids at home.

~ Your child was bullied in school and no one did anything about it, so you pulled him out.

~ Your child fell behind in school and remedial options were limited.

~ There's too much violence in schools and you're afraid your kids will get hurt.

~ Your school district has a bad reputation.

~ You don't like the subjects taught in public schools.

~ You believe it is a parent's duty to educate their own children.

~ Your child is advanced and doesn't get enough challenges in the public school system.

~ You can't afford private schooling.

~ Your family lifestyle is not conducive to school schedules. Some examples: managing a large family farm or other business, or having a job requiring a lot of travel.

~ You want your child to learn a different language or culture than what is taught in schools.

~ All of your friends are homeschooling and you felt peer pressure to homeschool, too.

~ Your spouse or a relative wants you to homeschool.

Distilling reasons into values

I have many different reasons for homeschooling. My son has Asperger's syndrome, a high-functioning form of autism. He does not do well in large, noisy groups, and he often has to pace while he's thinking. He learns best by discussing or by focusing on one topic and branching things out from that.

On the other hand, my daughter is neurotypical, but she's very active. If she can't move, stretch, stand on her hands, or jump, she starts to lose focus. She doesn't learn the same way as her brother does, but she also has trouble in a classroom setting because all that sitting is very hard for her.

I homeschool because I know a full, busy classroom would be difficult for both of them. I homeschool because I love being with them and exploring things with them. I homeschool because I know each of my children has special needs that I can cater to more easily than a teacher in a large classroom could. And I homeschool because I recognize giftedness in both of my children, and I don't want them to experience the bullying and boredom that I experienced in school.

Those aren't all my reasons for homeschooling, obviously, but from those paragraphs you can see a lot about what I value.

What I really want you to see is that there are a lot of different reasons why a family might choose to homeschool their children. When you are considering your values, please remember there are no right or wrong answers, and your answers might change from year to year. Right now, we're trying to discover what drives your intent to homeschool so we can make goals that will make sense for you.

If you value being at home with your children, then your goals will reflect your desire to be together as a family. If you value their being free from bullies, then your goals will emphasize a need to create a safe and kind environment for your children. If you value academics, your goals will focus on creating a challenging learning environment.

Now that you have listed several different reasons for homeschooling, we're going to try to distill those reasons into single words, phrases, or quotes that sum up your philosophy on home education. Your reasons reveal a lot about you and your values.

Let's look again at the reasons I gave for homeschooling. Do you see the things that are similar? I think you can find at least two of my values there.

One of my values is Creating a Learning Environment. Neither of my kids does well in a classroom setting. I'm sure they could get used to it if it were necessary, but I know they learn more in settings that celebrate their particular learning styles and preferences. Rather than forcing them into expectations of behavior that might be necessary for a large group, I give them the freedom they need to explore things, to pace around, or to do somersaults between math problems.

A second value you can see above is my belief in Personalized Education. While I teach both of my kids all the core subjects, I often teach them in very different ways. My son prefers traditional learning methods. He reads books, answer questions about what he has learned, and writes or draws his reactions. On the other hand, my daughter likes manipulatives, stories, pictures, and hands-on activities to help her understand concepts. I know she is learning when she incorporates a topic into her pretend play worlds.

Blueprint Sketch #3: Find the similarities.

Look through the lists of reasons you made in the first two sketch exercises. Which of your reasons are similar to one another? Are there reasons that can be grouped together? What are the big ideas that those reasons have in common with each other? Those common aspects are your big-picture values.

Fill in the blank: I value _____.

Values list

If you're having trouble coming up with words or phrases to define your values, try looking through this list to see if you connect with any of these. This list is not complete by any means, so if you come up with something that isn't on it, go with your thoughts.

~ Flexibility—You value being able to change things mid-stream and have time and energy for fun things that come up.

~ Personalized Education/Individuality—You value ensuring each of your children has a different educational experience based on their own strengths and weaknesses.

~ Family—You value being together as a family and caring for each other's needs.

~ Religious/Spiritual Freedom—You value teaching and practicing your family's religion and using religious curriculum and texts. On the opposite end, you could value freedom from religious pressure.

~ Real-World Training—You value learning specialized skills in a mentorship/internship model rather than the factory model of schooling. There are many examples of this, but a few include living on a farm, running a family business, or being an entertainer, performer, or athlete.

~ Hands-On Learning—You value getting your hands dirty and experimenting with things, and will forgo most textbook and worksheet work.

~ Parental Control over Education—You might value this one if you think that it is a parent's responsibility, and only a parent's responsibility, to raise a child.

~ Caring Environment—You value building up a child in a loving way and offering them freedom from bullying, teasing, competition, or harsh words.

~ Creativity—You value art projects, dressing up, acting out plays, learning songs, and drawing and painting. If you value creativity, you might frustrate yourself if you use a curriculum that is mostly textbooks and worksheets that stifle your creative expression.

~ Achievement—You value good grades, excellence in a sport or team activity, and/or winning awards in contests and tournaments. If achievement is one of your values, you're probably already thinking about college degrees and scholarships, and will have to plan accordingly starting as early as the elementary years.

~ Academics/Rigor in Education—If you value a rigorous education, you might be fond of the Classical model, and will likely teach difficult subjects because they are worth learning.

~ Interest-Led Learning—You value letting your children take the reins in their own educations. You would rather build around what they're interested in rather than stick to a strict curriculum.

~ Cultural Awareness—You value the big picture, so to speak; depending on what version of history you read, you might not get it. If you value cultural awareness, you'll want to teach about many different groups of people and how they do things in different ways.

~ Encouraging Independence and Self-Sufficiency—You value independence in your children, so you will probably have them doing a lot of things on their own from young ages, including chores, cooking, cleaning, or even running small businesses.

~ Safety—You value protecting your children from danger, whether physical, mental, emotional, or spiritual.

~ Health—Those who value health often have chronic health issues, allergies, or other needs that can best be treated by a parent as care-giver.

~ Lifelong Learning—If you value lifelong learning, you will tend to help your children learn how to learn, and then set them loose with the resources they need.

Define your top values

Maybe you're wondering why all this matters. Maybe you thought we'd get right into putting subjects on a calendar: "Math, 10:30 a.m., every weekday."

The truth is it's easy to lose sight of the things you think are most important when you're in the middle of a school year. You may say that Flexibility is one of your values, but in November you find yourself with such a tight schedule due to sporting events, holiday preparations, and other obligations that you want to pull your hair out. You may think that Family is a value, but if you and all of your kids each join a different activity, you might get frustrated that you're spending so much time in separate places. Or maybe you value Parental Control, but you signed up for that charter school or that government-run online school, and now they're telling you what curriculum you can or can't use. Setting your values will help you make those decisions before you make commitments you might regret.

I have my days when my value of Personalized Education gets thrown out the window. I start thinking, "My son was doing this thing at this age, so my daughter should be doing that, too." Or I think, "All my friends are using this curriculum, so I'm going to use it, too." I usually think that will make things easier, but it always ends in frustration for all of us. Why? Because I'm not acting according to my values. I'm actively going against something that I think is important.

If you don't clarify what's important to you, it's easy to go along with what others tell you to do. That can often lead to frustration if those things aren't a good fit for you and your family. So let's continue trying to nail down your values, so you have something to help you plan.

Blueprint Sketch #4: Define your top three values.

> Look through the list of values you just made, and pick two or three that you think are the Most Important. Write them down on a sheet of paper, or highlight them in your computer document.

We're going to focus on these top values for the rest of the planning in this book. It helps to have your values in mind for the next few steps, because those will drive your decisions on curriculum, goals, outside activities, and schedules. Your values might change from one year to another as you gain more experience as a homeschooler and as your children grow and mature. In the earlier years, Creativity was a top focus for me, but I can feel myself thinking more about Academics as the kids get older. I recommend going through this process every year before you start your planning to help you focus on what you think is most important at the time.

Make your values visible

This next step is optional, but I find it very helpful for me and my family. Discovering and articulating your values is a great start, but they gain exponential amounts of power when you make them visible.

If you've spent any amount of time on Pinterest, you've probably seen those painted signs that some people hang in their homes. They say things like, "In this house, we do real, we do mistakes, we say I'm sorry, we share laughter . . ." or "In this family, we use good manners, are kind and generous, act with integrity, forgive . . .". These are usually stenciled in large letters on big wooden signs, or across an entire wall. You can find several examples by running a search for "in this house" or "house rules" on Pinterest or in a Google search.

I love the idea behind these signs because they are large, visible reminders of the things that are important. These are over-sized values statements, made pretty with good fonts and aesthetically pleasing colors. Keeping your values highly visible in your home will ensure everyone knows them and can live by them during the year.

Blueprint Sketch #5: Choose a quote and make it visible.

> More than likely, a good quote or scripture came to your mind as you worked through the process of discovering your values. If that's the case, find it and write it down. Better yet, make a poster out of it and hang it on the wall. Write it in big letters on a white board. Make a graphic with it and turn it into your computer wallpaper. Have your kids help you make an artistic version of it that you can proudly hang on the refrigerator.

Several years ago, I found a graphic in a magazine that included a quote by Plato. It says, "The only real ill-doing is the deprivation of knowledge." Because that quote so closely connects with my philosophy of education, I've had it hanging on my refrigerator ever since. When I start getting crazy about whether I am teaching my kids well, I read it again. Sometimes it reminds me to tell the truth the best I can, even for a difficult subject (this helped tremendously when we had several deaths in the family in one year). Other times, it reminds me that I'm already doing a fantastic job of imparting as much knowledge to them as I can.

Another quote I have loved for many years is from the book *Learning All the Time* by John Holt. "Real learning is a process of discovery, and if we want it to happen, we must create the kinds of conditions in which discoveries are made. We know what these are. They include time, leisure, freedom, and a lack of pressure."

That quote has brought me down from the ledge more than a few times. I tend to lose my focus in the middle of winter and start pushing for more book work, more reading, and more worksheets to prove we are good homeschoolers. Then I read that quote again and remember that I can read all the books and teach all the things I've ever known, but the kids won't learn anything if they aren't receptive and discovering things for themselves. It reminds me to back off and let them be scientists: observing, making guesses about what they'll see, experimenting with different outcomes, then truly learning something new about their world. It doesn't just work in science. It also works in history, in social studies, in health, in chores and work, and even in math.

If you're not familiar with John Holt, he was a retired educator who is often considered the father of the unschooling movement. Unschooling is a philosophy of education in which children direct their own learning and experiences without any forced schedules or plans. The idea is that children are born curious and will learn the things they want and need to know without too much trouble. I don't consider myself a true unschooler (or I wouldn't be writing a book about planning!), but I do use many unschooling ideas in my homeschool. Even though the quote is from a source on one end of the homeschooling spectrum, it still speaks to me where I am and reminds me of what I think is important.

Those are just a few examples of quotes that help me define my values. Keeping them visible gives me a boost when I start feeling discouraged.

Do you have a quote or scripture that you can use to remind you why you do what you do? Here are some quotes that might be relevant to your homeschool philosophy, and might be worth hanging on your walls as a reminder when you need it.

Quotes

Achievement:

"Learning is not attained by chance. It must be sought for with ardor and attended to with diligence." -*Abigail Adams*

"Education is not received. It is achieved." -*unknown*

"There are no shortcuts to any place worth going." -*Beverly Sills*

Creativity:

"It is the supreme art of the teacher to awaken joy in creative expression and knowledge." -*Albert Einstein*

"Imagination is more important than knowledge. Knowledge is limited. Imagination encircles the world." -*Albert Einstein*

Lifelong Learning:

"The mind is not a vessel to be filled, but a fire to be kindled." -*Plutarch*

"If you want to build a ship, don't herd people together to collect wood and don't assign them tasks and work but rather,

teach them to long for the endless immensity of the sea."
-*Antoine de Saint-Exupery*

"Education is a process of living and not a preparation for future living." -*John Dewey*

"Learn from yesterday, live for today, hope for tomorrow. The important thing is not to stop questioning." -*Albert Einstein*

Literacy:

"Frederick Douglass taught that literacy is the path from slavery to freedom. There are many kinds of slavery and many kinds of freedom, but reading is still the path." -*Carl Sagan*

"A person who won't read has no advantage over one who can't read." -*Mark Twain*

Individualized Education:

"Everybody is a genius. But if you judge a fish by its ability to climb a tree, it will live its whole life believing that it is stupid." -*Albert Einstein*

"If a child can't learn the way we teach, maybe we should teach the way they learn." -*Ignacio Estrada*

Educating the Whole Person:

"Educating the mind without educating the heart is no education at all." -*Aristotle*

Relaxed Education/Unschooling:

"Real learning is a process of discovery, and if we want it to happen, we must create the kinds of conditions in which discoveries are made. We know what these are. They include time, leisure, freedom, and a lack of pressure." -*John Holt*

"I never teach my pupils. I only provide the conditions in which they can learn." -*Albert Einstein*

Self-Sufficiency:

"Never help a child with a task at which he feels he can succeed." -*Maria Montessori*

"You cannot help men permanently by doing for them what they could do for themselves." -*Abraham Lincoln*

The Role of a Teacher:

"The only real ill-doing is the deprivation of knowledge." -*Plato*

"If you are planning for a year, sow rice; if you are planning for a decade, plant trees; if you are planning for a lifetime, educate people." -*Chinese proverb*

"By teaching you will learn. By learning you will teach." -*Latin proverb*

"The best teachers are those who show you where to look, but don't tell you what to see." -*Alexandra K. Trenfor*

Parental Involvement:

"If a child is to keep alive his inborn sense of wonder, he needs the companionship of at least one adult who can share it, rediscovering with him the joy, excitement, and mystery of the world we live in." -*Rachel Carson*

"Tell me and I'll forget; show me and I may remember; involve me and I'll understand." -*Chinese proverb*

World Citizenry:

"Don't think of the world you leave your children, think of the children you leave the world." -*Unknown*

"If we are to teach real peace in this world, and if we are to carry on a real war against war, we shall have to begin with the children." -*Mahatma Gandhi*

"Education is the most powerful weapon you can use to change the world." -*Nelson Mandela*

Religious Education:

"And these words that I command you today shall be on your heart. You shall teach them diligently to your children, and shall talk of them when you sit in your house, and when you walk by the way, and when you lie down, and when you rise." -*Deuteronomy 6:6-7, ESV*

"Train up a child in the way he should go; even when he is old he will not depart from it." -*Proverbs 22:6, ESV*

"The object of education is not merely to enable our children to gain their daily bread and to acquire pleasant means of recreation, but that they should know God and serve Him with earnestness and devotion." -*Hermann Adler*

Final notes on values

Once you've found a quote that you like, create something with it. If you'd rather use a single word or phrase, there are plenty of ways to make those visible, too. Many craft stores sell wooden letters that you can paint, decoupage, or decorate to your heart's content. Stencils are an easy way to add quotes to walls, paper, or T-shirts. And lest you think you have to be super artsy about it, I confess that the John Holt quote I mentioned was scribbled in my terrible handwriting and hung on a magnetic white board on my fridge for several years. I never made it pretty; I just made it visible. As long as you see it often and it serves as a reminder to you, you can do it in whatever style best works for you.

Beware: If you make your values visible, your kids or spouse might call you out when you start doing things that conflict with those values. These reminders might come when you're frustrated and grouchy, and you might not like it. Keep an open mind, though, and you might see a pattern like I did. You might see that you are at your worst when you're going against your values. All that frustration is usually a result of losing sight of what's most important. Having someone else point it out can help you get back on track and ease those feelings of angst.

If your children help you choose and display your values, you'll see another benefit: they'll feel more involved and responsible for their own education and will often work harder as a result. My kids know what I'm trying to do, and they know what makes our homeschool special. When it comes time to do some of the harder parts of it, they can talk themselves through those "I don't wanna!" feelings, and they know why it's important to work hard. Even when my children were very small, they liked being a part of the brainstorming sessions about our values. Their values often consisted of things like "Dessert at every meal!" and "More play time!" I learned not to laugh off these suggestions. Making life sweeter and having more fun can be great values.

Values review

In this section, we've talked about reasons for homeschooling, narrowed down two or three core values that drive your desire to educate at home, and then made those values visible so you can be reminded of them throughout your year. If you have successfully completed this section, congratulations! You now have a better idea about what's most important to you and your family as you homeschool.

Some of you may have loved this section, but please don't stop there. You've managed the equivalent of choosing where in the world you want to live. Now, we're going to start planning what kind of house we're going to build.

For those who would rather get to the nitty-gritty of calendar planning, we're getting there! But just like the Bible story about the foolish man building his house on sand, you don't want to start planning without having a purpose in mind. Set your values first, and the rest will make more sense.

Review Questions

~ Why do you homeschool? What parts of education at home are the most important to you? Make a list of reasons you choose to educate at home.

~ What part of homeschooling would you miss if you had to give it up? What things would be hard to do if you weren't homeschooling? On the other hand, what things might be easier if you weren't homeschooling? What are some of the things you are giving up in order to homeschool?

~ What do your kids and spouse or other family members like about homeschooling? What do they dislike? Talking with them will help you narrow down your values or give you fresh ideas.

~ What are the ideas that all your lists have in common? Out of the things you like and the things you dislike, can you find some core ideas that define why you choose to educate at home? Usually there is a word or phrase to describe the overarching thought or feeling for several ideas.

~ Choose two or three of these big ideas to be your values for your school year.

~ Find a phrase, quote, scripture, or list that encompasses those big picture values for you. Create a sign or poster and hang it somewhere visible. This will help your whole family stay focused on the important things as you work through your homeschool year.

Part Two: Methods

Plums, 10¢

A few summers ago my son, James, decided he was going to start a business. He was probably four years old at the time, right at that age when the most common utterance out of his mouth was, "Do it myself!"

We had a large bush full of Indian plums in the backyard. Indian plums are about the size of almonds, and even though they are edible, they are somewhat bitter. Natives used to use them for tea and medicinal purposes, but they're not the type of thing you'd snack on by the handful during the summer months. They're probably similar to dandelions—you know you can eat them, but nobody really does.

James decided he was going to sell the plums. I tried to offer him some alternate ideas.

"Why don't you try a lemonade stand? It's a nice day for it," I suggested.

He refused. "Plums," he said.

"How about paintings? You could sell some of the art you've done recently," I recommended.

"No."

I found it quite amusing and decided to let him do it his own way.

He gathered a small bowl full of the plums he'd picked. He found a small table and dragged it into the back yard. He made a sign, "Plums, 10¢," and placed it carefully on his table. He took out a chair, one of those small plastic ones that goes with a Little Tikes table, and then he sat.

He was a very patient little fellow. He sat there at his little table, facing the chain link fence that separated our backyard from the neighbor's backyard, and waited.

He sat patiently for over an hour. He waited for customers to arrive who would buy his tiny plums for ten cents each. No one came.

I bet you can think of a few reasons his plum-selling business didn't take off. For one, he set up his shop where no one would find it. If he had set up his table in the front yard by the road, someone might have stopped by. However, even if he had set up in a better location, he probably would not have had many sales because the thing he was trying to sell had no value.

He did everything right, though, and he worked very hard at it. He carefully gathered all his plums, ripe or not, to sell them. He set up the table with his large sign and his nice bowl. He sat patiently and waited for his customers, rather than abandoning the idea moments later.

I think a lot of homeschoolers are like my son—trying to sell things no one really wants where there are no customers. I know I was when I first started. If all your attempts to teach out of a frustrating textbook are being met with tears, it might be time to double-check your methods.

Intro to methods

One of the first things new homeschoolers usually ask me is, "What curriculum should I use?" If you've been homeschooling for a while, you know this is a loaded question. For one, there are so many different options available that it's not easy in a quick conversation to cover even a tiny percentage of them. Second, it completely depends on the parent and the children involved.

For many homeschoolers, the preferred method of teaching is a missing piece of the puzzle. We can spend a long time looking for the "right" curriculum without really knowing what will work best for our particular needs. When that popular curriculum that your best friend adores ends up failing you, you might start thinking that frustration is part of the homeschool life or you might wonder whether you were truly meant to homeschool at all.

Save yourself the heartache. There are many ways to educate your children.

I have a wonderful friend who was born to be an early elementary educator. She is the embodiment of fun. She loves crafts. She loves dramas and skits and costumes and music. She and her kids regularly have theme days where they wear historical clothes, eat foods from various cultures, and play games from different time periods. They do a lot of crafts, drawings, and art projects that go along with their studies. She once covered her entire wall with a hand-torn construction paper map of Africa. She posts pictures online of her kids' amazing and creative projects.

She and I are very different. As much as I love her, my first response to most of her posts is, "I need a nap just looking at this." I am not a high-energy person. I've put in my days of big, beautiful projects, and I've come out of it with a severe dislike of glitter and a lot of paper cuts. To me, those projects tend to be more work than they are worth. I love books and stories and pretend play, but I tend to keep things as simple as I can. Our school day might consist of a few hours of reading and discussing things together, and then I let the kids loose to express themselves however they will.

I admire my friend's methods, though. On some of my worst days, I see her wonderful hard work and feel jealous that she seems to be having so much fun. Sometimes I even feel a little worthless, like I'm not doing enough to earn my homeschool stripes.

Do you ever feel like that? Do you ever look at another homeschool parent and feel like you're not doing enough?

The best way I know to combat those feelings is two-fold: first, I have to recognize that other families learn in different ways than mine, and second, I have to be confident that I'm doing the things that work best in my family. If you know how you operate best, it will save you from the despair of wondering if you're doing it wrong.

How do you figure out the things that work best in your family? In this section, I'll present several different homeschool methods and ideas, and ask you a series of questions. I'll present the common answers that go along with popular methods or philosophies so you can figure out what might work best for you. This will be a rough overview, and won't go into every possible method or type of curriculum, but it should give you a good place to start. It will also help you see how many different ways there are to approach educational issues.

As you go through the following exercises, keep in mind that you might not find the perfect method or style for your needs. This is only an overview. You may need to mix-and-match various methods to get the results you want. You might even end up using something you didn't think you would like because you like the people or community or because it works better than anything else. That happens a lot, too.

For now, let's look through the different types of methods for different educational philosophies, teaching styles, learning styles, and evaluations. That will help you narrow down your curriculum choices for the next part.

Educational philosophy

One of the first things you'll need to figure out is your own philosophy of education. That might sound complex, but it really just refers to what you think of when you think of education. Not everyone has the same ideas about what education is for. Some people think education means the ability to recite a lot of facts and do difficult math problems. Others think it refers to what kinds of books you have read. Still others might think education is about living life as a kind and generous person.

What kind of educational style fits your values best? Here are a few sketches to help you get started.

Blueprint Sketch #6: Imagine your ideal school day.

> If you could create the most perfect school day for your children, what would it look like? Where would you be? What kinds of activities would you be doing? How involved would you, the teacher, be?

Depending on your answers to those questions, we can start narrowing down your preferences and finding you some new ideas.

See if any of these answers fits your ideal school day.

1. "We should be exploring the outdoors as much as possible! Kids learn best when they are outside in nature."

   ~ If this idea is for you, you might work best with a Charlotte Mason style of education.

2. "Our school day should look as much like 'real life' as possible. We should be working together and learning in real life situations. You can learn math at the grocery store better than you can with worksheets."

~ If this sounds good to you, you might enjoy unschooling.

3. "Kids learn best when they're given structure and a routine, and when they're taught in the way people have always been taught. They should read classic texts, memorize facts, copy great writing, and work hard every day to learn."

~ This is Classical Education at its best.

4. "Books! We should be surrounded by books that are fun to read and are written from many different perspectives. Textbooks are boring. Real books are the way to learn."

~ If you love picture books, historical fiction, and stories that teach concepts in a fun way, then you might believe in a living books style of learning. Sonlight is one of the major providers of this type of curriculum, but it also fits with a Charlotte Mason style of education (see #1).

5. "We should play! Kids learn best while playing, pretending, and using toys and hands-on experiments that help them experience an idea."

~ Montessori education might be your favorite. You might also enjoy unit studies.

6. "Why should I teach, when there are so many experts available online and through DVDs? I'd rather have the kids on the computer, where they can track what they're learning and the kids can work at their own pace."

~ If this sounds appealing to you, you'll want to look into online learning, Open Learning, or computer-based learning methods.

7. "I want my kids' school experience to be like mine. They should have their own desks, textbooks to work through, and they should learn the same subjects their peers are learning at this age."

~ This is sometimes referred to as "School at Home" and basically means keeping it as similar to schools as possible. A Beka is a type of curriculum used in both Christian schools and homeschools. Homeschoolers can also purchase many different types of curricula that are used in regular schools. I use several of the worktexts from Evan Moor, for instance, which local schools use as well.

8. "I like everything mentioned above! I want to mix-and-match my favorite parts of all of them. I don't want to be stuck in one style or another."

~ If this was your response to the other answers, you're probably an Eclectic Homeschooler. Take heart! You're not alone. The myriad of options available make it easy for us to mix-and-match styles to create a customized education for our children.

These are just a few of the options to get you started. If none of these fit you, that's okay. Research any of them that sound interesting to you and just define your own perfect day. It will help as you choose curriculum in later sections.

Teaching style

If you're just starting out, you might not know how you will manage your time and subjects yet. I am often asked how I choose what to teach during the year, both by homeschoolers and by curious bystanders. It's a difficult question. Will you branch out on your own and teach whatever you and your kids are curious about? Or will you stick to the local public school curicululum as closely as possible?

This section will help you narrow down some of those options.

Blueprint Sketch #7: How will you manage what you're teaching?

> Knowing whether you prefer Classical education or unschooling is a good start. There are still a lot of options for curriculum within those philosophies. Let's narrow things down a bit more and talk about your teaching and management style. How will you decide what to teach and when?

1. "I don't decide! Give me a schedule that tells me what to do and when to do it, and I'll be happy."

   ~ If this is you, you're in great company. There are many different retailers of pre-boxed curricula, like Sonlight, Timberdoodle, or A Beka, that will keep you on track.

2. "I like having options to choose from, but I don't want to have to come up with too much on my own."

   ~ You might do best with Unit Studies, textbooks, or living books programs that are pre-written.

3. "I'll go by whatever the standards say to do."

~ The Common Core standards are available to print for free online. You can reference those during your year. The *What Your ___th Grader Needs to Know* books might be helpful for you as well.

4. "I'd rather let my kids learn things they're interested in. I'm happy to find books and projects for them based on what they like."

~ If interest-led learning is in your cards, get a library card and make sure you have constant Internet access to help you find good resources.

5. "I like to plan my own curricula for certain subjects, because there's nothing out there that is exactly what I want."

~ Many educators create their own curricula. Classical educators often tie everything into the four-year history cycle and plan their school year around that. However you choose to do it, if you're a do-it-yourself type, you're not alone.

6. "I want to focus on one subject or book each month, and center our learning around that."

~ If you prefer the Unit Studies approach, you might enjoy using Five in a Row or similar curriculum options. Often, you can find pre-planned units that tell you what to do, but you get to decide which unit to use and when.

Learning styles

All your favorite curricula in the world won't do a thing if you're using it with a child who can't learn from it. I have a friend who absolutely adores Waldorf education, which is a style that is built on exploration and hands-on crafts and pretend play. When she first started homeschooling, she purchased all sorts of wonderful supplies and dreamed of using them with her kids.

To her chagrin, neither of her kids really took to the Waldorf style. She did her best, but discovered that her son did better by learning from audiobooks and traditional teaching. She still has those lovely supplies and pulls them out sometimes just to admire them. Many in my homeschool community share similar stories. Homeschool parents have a curriculum they fall in love with, but it just doesn't work with their kids. Part of this has to do with a child's learning style and how they prefer to gather information.

Blueprint Sketch #8: What's your child's learning style?

This can be hard to figure out when your children are very small, but as they get older, you can often recognize a strength in one style or another. How do your kids learn information best? How do they remember things?

1. "My child learns best from reading books or looking at pictures. Sometimes, it seems as though they are looking at a video in their mind when they try to remember something. They notice details in picture books and can quickly find something in a book they read."

~Visual learners tend to absorb most of their information through their eyes. These types of learners are often good readers and will enjoy having pictures and text available to learn from. Many of the more traditional methods of learning, like textbooks and worksheets, will work well with visual learners.

2. "My child likes to listen to music and audiobooks. They will sometimes make up songs to remember things. They can remember and follow spoken directions. They prefer to be read to out loud and will sometimes talk to themselves or make noises as they do difficult tasks."

~ Auditory learners absorb information through their ears. They prefer to be told how to do something rather than read it in a book. Your auditory learner will learn from being read to and from the things you say to them. Audiobooks, music, and videos with narration might be some of their favorite ways to learn.

3. "My child likes to do things. They are constantly on the move and I often have to ask them to sit down or stop fiddling when I'm trying to tell them something. They love hands-on projects and often have no patience to listen to directions—they just want to dive right in to whatever we're doing."

~Kinesthetic learners learn best through movement and by doing. These are the people who throw away the directions and figure things out for themselves. A kinesthetic learner will often need to move around as they are learning or recalling information. Kinesthetic learners are often fiddlers and doodlers. It might appear that they are not paying attention to you, when they are actually doing exactly what they need to in order to be able to recall what you're teaching. If you have a kinesthetic learner, they'll probably enjoy a lot of art and craft projects and will enjoy acting out the things they are learning.

Knowing your child's learning style might help you narrow down your choices. I've presented only one theory of learning styles. There are several others out there. I highly recommend doing more research on learning styles and multiple intelligences if this is an area that interests you. Just keep in mind that finding the right fit might take a bit of trial-and-error. When it comes to learning styles, I try to teach to all three. My son seems to be a visual learner, and my daughter is a mix of auditory and kinesthetic. However, I think they both learn best by seeing, hearing, *and* doing. Isolating methods might work best for a child who is very strong in one of the learning styles, but I would caution you against catering too strongly to only one style.

Curriculum types

When it comes time to shop for curriculum, you will discover that there are a lot of options out there. Based on your own teaching style and your child's learning style, you might want to decide what kind of resources you want to use to teach. In my case, I use a variety of many of these, but you might decide that one or the other fits better with you and your family.

Blueprint Sketch #9: Find your curriculum type.

> In your ideal school, what types of resources would your children be using in order to learn? What types of things would you be using to teach?

1. "The child should read a chapter of a textbook, then do the review questions and worksheets related to the text. Textbooks and worksheets should be from trusted curriculum writers."

   ~ If it's easiest for you to follow a pre-scripted curriculum, then you're in luck. There are plenty of great options from many different perspectives. Find textbooks that you think would work best with your style.

2. "The child should read story books, picture books, and lots of nonfiction works about the various school subjects."

   ~ If you're a living book learner (books that are not textbooks), then you'll probably use the library often, or will need a lot of space for bookshelves! If this is you, check out the Sonlight and Rainbow Resource catalogs for ideas for books that fit your subjects.

3. "My kids should watch DVDs and online videos, play computer games and phone apps, and do reviews on the computer. It's really fun and easy that way."

~ If this is the method that would work best for you and your child, then you might enjoy Switched-On Schoolhouse, Teaching Textbooks, Khan Academy, or other computer-based learning resources.

4. "I think we should do a lot of hands-on experiments, projects, and crafts. It's not learning if you're not getting your hands dirty!"

~ If this is your style, you will probably enjoy looking through the Timberdoodle and Home Science Tools catalogs for good resources. I'd also recommend the Williamson Kids Can series of books, which always include hands-on projects and experiments in many different subjects.

5. "True education doesn't require any special resources or curriculum. Real life and everyday experiences are enough to learn from."

~ Unschooling is probably the most frugal option for homeschooling, although I suspect you'll collect just as many school supplies as the rest of us do.

6. "Kids should memorize facts, copy great works, and study classical languages, literature, and philosophy."

~ If you are a Classical educator, you'll probably want to own a copy of The Well-Trained Mind by Susan Wise Bauer, and you could benefit from being part of the Classical Conversations community.

Evaluation

If you've followed educational news at all in the last few years, you know that standardized testing is a polarizing issue. It seems to be one of the necessary evils of schools, and one of the few ways to answer the question, "Are kids learning what we're trying to teach?"

Depending on where you live, standardized testing might be a requirement for homeschoolers. In Washington State, all homeschoolers, age 8 and above, have to take a yearly standardized test or have an evaluation done by a certified teacher. In California, standardized tests are not a requirement for private schools, but many of the charter schools that homeschoolers belong to will require testing in order for your child to participate in the program. Double-check your legal requirements before you get too far into this section.

This section is not just about the yearly standardized tests, but about keeping track of what and how your child is learning throughout the year. How will you evaluate whether they've learned what you're teaching?

Blueprint Sketch #10: What's testing got to do with it?

> Where do you fall on the testing spectrum? Do you believe in keeping grades for your kids and doing a lot of quizzes and tests? What kinds of records do you keep? Do you have another method of evaluating what they've learned and what they know?

1. "The kids take tests and I give honest grades on homework. The child must complete these things alone, and pass, or it's cheating."

~ This is the standardized model and philosophy on evaluation. If this works best for you, it's most likely that you'll also prefer using traditional textbooks and worksheets.

2. "If they miss something on their work, I reteach it to make sure they understand, and let them fix it until it's correct."

~ For you, the errors only help you see what the child doesn't understand. You believe in revising and reteaching anything that is incorrect.

3. "The kids give reports or write papers to show what they are learning."

~ This would be a response style of evaluation, and great for homeschoolers who need to keep a portfolio of work for review. Homeschoolers who do a lot of notebooking are using this style of evaluation.

4. "I just know what the kids are learning, because I can tell from daily work and discussions that they understand it."

~ This is an evaluation style based on relationship, and it's one of the strengths of one-on-one teaching in a homeschool. If you're around your children all the time, you know what kinds of things they are learning.

5. "The kids take whatever tests are required by law. Besides, it's good practice for future testing like the SAT."

~ In this case, you probably do the tests, but don't worry too much about the results. That's another benefit to homeschooling: our jobs don't depend on our children doing well on their tests. On the other hand, flexibility in teaching styles and one-on-one education might mean our children do well on tests anyway.

6. "I have an outside evaluator come in once a week/month/year to assess my children's work and make sure we're on track. It's better to have someone from outside the family tell me what I might be missing so we can fill in any gaps."

~ I know of many families who do periodic evaluations this way, usually with a certified teacher. This type of evaluation can often reveal any issues your child has and can give you new ideas for how to do things in the future. This is especially effective for children with special needs or a child who would not do well with the pressure of a testing environment.

Again, you might use several of these methods during your year. Ultimately, it's up to you to decide how you plan to manage evaluation and testing, as long as you are within your legal requirements as a homeschooler. Many places with legal testing requirements will have group testing options or will allow you to take your child to the school to participate during their testing periods. You can also use one of the online programs that let you administer the test at home and then send it in for scoring.

Methods review

No matter where you fit on the spectrum of homeschoolers, you'll find plenty of resources to support your style of education. Just be honest with yourself and do what works best for you in your situation. Don't try to be a strict school-at-home educator if your true strength is in hands-on learning and exploration.

On the other hand, don't feel like you have to adopt an entire system just because you like parts of it. I like to call myself a Classical unschooler, which is a paradox. Everything I do is based on teaching world history chronologically, one thing after another, in a four-year repeating cycle. However, my actual teaching style looks a lot more like a Charlotte Mason education. I love living books, we constantly spend time exploring our environment, and much of our school day looks very relaxed. In fact, my way of teaching the history cycle is almost more like an interest-led unit study: we find books on whatever topics seem interesting based on where we are in history.

Why am I spending so much time talking about methods? Because yearly goals can often revolve around finishing a particular level of curriculum or studying a particular subject. If you're using materials that don't really work for you (even if they work for your friend or everyone in an online forum), you'll be less likely to meet your goals. Once you know your ideal process, it will be much easier to pick and choose curriculum you'll actually enjoy rather than purchasing a lot of materials and feeling regretful that they gather dust on your shelves.

Regardless of what you end up using and how you go about your school day, I think you'll find that you can still get along quite well with other homeschoolers who are doing things differently. The two homeschool co-ops I've been in have always contained a large variety of parents with different methods and philosophies. I think it's beneficial having the Classical Conversations mom around to remind you how to diagram sentences, or the Montessori mom who knows how to get kids to do chores, or the creative mom who will take on the arduous task of leading a theater group of your ragtag bunch of homeschool kids.

I say all this because I don't want you to feel like you will be alone as a homeschooler if you choose XYZ curriculum and everyone else is using ABC curriculum. There is plenty of overlap. Find the methods that you believe in and that fit your values, and you will have much greater success and satisfaction.

If you haven't yet, take a moment to answer these questions:

~ What does your ideal school day look like? What kinds of resources and activities would you like to use for learning? Would you prefer to have a small school in your home, or would you rather fit schooling in wherever it fits in your life?

~ How do you choose what resources you will use for teaching? Do you prefer to have everything written out for you, or do you like to come up with some of it yourself? Will you use textbooks or online learning or will you go with what the kids are interested in?

~ How do your children tend to learn best? Are they strong in a particular learning style, like visual, auditory, or kinesthetic learning?

~ What kinds of activities do you want your children to be doing each day? Do you want them working through textbooks and worksheets, reading storybooks that introduce subjects, or memorizing facts and copying the classical masters?

~ How will you evaluate what your child has learned? Will you do tests and quizzes? Will you keep grades? Are you required to do standardized testing?

Now, keep those answers in mind as you search for your ideal curriculum and start setting goals for your upcoming school year.

Part Three: Setting Goals

Long-term goals

"What do you want to be when you grow up?" This has to be the most common question asked of small children. And they usually know, don't they? My kids know what they want to be. My son wants to be a video game designer. My daughter wants to be a wildlife biologist.

These dreams change often. Two years ago, my son was determined to become an entomologist and study insects for a living, especially caterpillars and butterflies. My daughter wanted to be a chef.

What do your kids want to be? What kinds of things are they interested in? For the sake of goal-setting, we're going to run with those dreams and see what helpful things we can discover. While it's not possible to look into the future, it can still be fun to imagine what our kids might be like as adults. If you can imagine the possibilities, the steps to achieving that future might become more clear.

I have friends who are very good at sports: soccer, basketball, baseball, and fast-pitch softball. Even though their children are still quite young, they have done everything they can to give their kids a boost in sports. They've changed schools. They've created their own local basketball league so they can travel to tournaments. They coach and attend all sorts of camps. Why do they do all this? They believe sports will give their children better lives via networking, college scholarships, good health, and opportunities.

Even if you're not thinking of college, you've likely considered your own ideas of success for your children when they become adults. We're going to take those ideas and craft a long-term vision for your child's education.

Please keep one thing in mind as you do this exercise: these are your dreams for your child. Until your kids can offer their input, you'll be extrapolating based on your child's individual strengths and weaknesses. This isn't set in stone, though. You don't want to lock your child into a life trajectory she can't escape from, or you'll both feel disappointed. Try to separate your own dreams from your child's abilities, too. It may be your dream to have a sporty child, but if you have a child who spends her time in the outfield making dandelion crowns and telling stories to bees, you might get frustrated. For this section, try to imagine what your child would love to do, and we'll probably come up with a great plan.

Envisioning a future

Have you ever looked at your kids and imagined what they might be like as adults? It can be hard to imagine sometimes, since they were just born a week or two ago! If any of the grandparents I know are right, it will feel like just another week before they're grown and gone. It can be easy to get bogged down in the day-to-day reality and lose sight of the bigger picture of our role in raising adults. Trying to imagine what your child will be like ten years from now can adjust your focus and help you see what choices you could be making right now. Times will obviously change a lot between now and then and there will be many variables outside of your control, but it's good to get an idea of what kind of adult you're hoping to educate.

Blueprint Sketch #11: Envision the future.

> Let's start with a few questions about your child. If you have more than one, answer the questions separately for each of

them. Exploring the answers with a spouse, your child's grandparents, or even the child himself may give you a clearer picture than what you can come up with on your own. Keep in mind that some of these questions can be difficult to answer when a child is very young. That's okay.

1. What is your child interested in? What does your child do when there's free time?
2. What is your child good at?
3. What could you see your child doing as a fully grown and independent adult, based on their current interests?
4. What types of things are hard for your child?
5. What do you think your child would be happy doing as an adult?

I'll give you some examples and show you how I might answer these questions for my kids.

My son is a Minecraft addict. He spends most of his free time playing the game, reading the wiki, watching mod showcases and Let's Plays on YouTube, and managing our family server. He has an idea for a mod of the game that he would like to create. Based on that, and his many years building levels and experimenting in various games, I can imagine him being on a game development team. (Last year, I imagined him working in a chemistry lab. Interests can and will fluctuate often.)

My son gets overwhelmed in loud or very busy places, much like I do. Because of that, he would probably work best in a quiet, self-directed environment. It is also hard for him to communicate in a large group or to speak up so that others can hear and listen to him. Those things might make it difficult for him in a highly competitive design environment, or in a place where he needs to be able to take the initiative and explain what he's doing. Knowing that these are weaknesses, I can help him learn those skills now, before they become a problem area.

I think my son would be happy designing games, playing games, and reviewing games for others. In general terms, I know he'd also like to have a happy and stable home life where he is loved and understood and can bounce his ideas off others.

Having that overview can help me think through some of the skills he could be working on this year to get closer to those goals.

Need another example? My daughter's main areas of interest are art and wildlife biology. She is the girl who started drawing as soon as she could hold a crayon. She recently told me that if she were a *My Little Pony* character, her "cutie mark" would be a pencil and sketchbook. (If you're not familiar with the show, each character has a cutie mark, or a symbol that shows their main gift or interest.)

My daughter spends hours making colorful, detailed drawings of the things that interest her. She also has quite a collection of bird-watching supplies, including binoculars and local bird identification guides. When she sees a new bird, she will quickly draw a detailed picture of it, and then try to find it in one of her books. I can imagine her as an illustrator or graphic designer or possibly a zoologist.

Math is not her favorite subject, and she tends to lose track of time and get distracted easily. For her, a creative and flexible environment would work best. She is also very soft-spoken and prone to being manipulated because she is very kind, so I would want to help her be more self-assured, especially if her arts career led her to freelancing.

Next steps

Now that you have that image in mind of your child as a successful adult, we're going to do another exercise. Even though this might seem like a lot, it shouldn't take very long. If your children are still quite young, this might be too much to consider at the moment. Feel free to skim or skip this step.

Let's think through your child's future education. Do you think your child will need a college education in order to get their ideal future job? It's never too early to ask this question, because you'll need to save up and you'll have to cater several years of education to this particular goal. If college is a likely requirement, will that change what you need to do this year to prepare?

If college is not a future goal, are there other types of alternative education that you can prepare for? For instance, there are mentorship or apprenticeship programs available for many different job and career types. Entrepreneurs can often benefit from networking with other entrepreneurs.

Depending on your child's goals and current school level, are there certain subjects they will have to learn in high school? Some colleges have subject requirements for entrance, such as a number of years of math, science, and foreign languages. There are also vocational programs and opportunities for high schoolers whose career goals do not require university degrees.

If you're not close to high school yet, are there ways you can help your child prepare now? Can you teach study skills and independent life skills that will make their future education go more smoothly?

Blueprint Sketch #12: Break it down.

> Considering all the ideas you thought through in the above paragraphs, is there anything specific you can do this year to help your child get closer to that dream of successful adulthood?

Most of this might sound very career-based, but it doesn't have to be. Much of what constitutes a successful, self-sufficient adult won't be written into your standardized testing. If your goal is to raise a tenderhearted adult who cares for the needs of others, now is your chance to develop those traits in your five-year-old. If you want your child to be a self-driven adult, find ways to offer practice at those skills now.

Let me show you how I break my ideals down into workable steps. My son, the video game programmer, has some options. The best scenario would be to get him into a college for game design and/or computer science. The second best scenario would be to get him some business training and let him become an independent game designer. In either case, there are steps he should take to get there.

He'll need a strong background in math. In fact, if I can get him through calculus, he has a greater chance of doing well with the physics of video game mechanics. Physics is important, too, meaning he'll need to learn the majority of the sciences at a high level. Being able to do the complex math means he should get a head start on understanding algebra and the basics of addition, subtraction, multiplication, and division should be second nature to him.

A firm basis in language and logic is in order, as are good typing and computer skills. If he'll be making games, he should also know something about classic stories and archetypes, psychology, and sociology.

Now, I could probably get all that from reading Common Core standards, but I wouldn't have such a strong reason to be sure I taught my son all those different subjects. I would be teaching them because some list said I should, not because they could be useful or interesting for my son's future. Now I have more incentive to teach the boy how to type, how to balance an algebraic equation, and how to understand the logic of computer languages.

How would that look for my daughter? She has a lot of interests, but there are two important things I know: she expresses herself best with drawing, and she loves nature and animals. If she were to go on to be an artist or illustrator, she'd need a lot of time to practice and a good background in art appreciation and varying styles. If she were to go into wildlife biology, she'd need a firm basis in science, especially anatomy and zoology. Her artistic abilities could be of excellent use as a naturalist, so finding her a good art mentor and teaching her the techniques of drawing what she sees will be helpful.

If she's going to be a self-sufficient adult, she'll need to know consumer math at least. Since math is not her strongest or most favorite subject, I realized I needed to switch the math curriculum to something that used a lot of concrete, real-world examples. She is now using the Life of Fred series and supplementing with Khan Academy and she adores it. Being able to do good design also means a strong background in geometry, so focusing on geometry as a core math subject can be good for her.

Due to the amount of time she spends practicing drawing, I keep the house stocked with the highest quality art supplies I can afford. I let her draw as part of her science, history, and math lessons. Her interest in biology also drives my desire to teach basic Latin and Greek roots in early elementary.

Do you see how different my kids are? I only have two of them! If you have more kids, you probably already know how different they all can be. In all honesty, my kids learn the same things together for 85% of each school day, despite the fact that they are in different grades. The only things I really change are the ways I evaluate whether they've learned or not.

Please don't be afraid of dreaming big here. You may look at all this and think, "Who in the world has time to focus that much?" Obviously, Personalized Education is a value of mine, so I may personalize things more than you would. If you don't want to do this for each and every child, you can also get a more generalized picture and apply it across the board. Instead of all the questions about college and future education, simply ask yourself, "What kind of adult do I hope to raise? What life skills should an adult person have, in my opinion?"

Your answers to that can help you narrow down your focus now.

If you haven't already, take some time to think through what you imagine your child's future education will require before you move on to the next section.

The law and Common Core

One of the first things I do before setting my yearly goals is to double-check my local homeschool laws. In some places, there are very particular things you have to do in order to homeschool, including listing your yearly curriculum and providing portfolios for review. In other places, it's as simple as filling out a form to let the state know your kids will be home with you. Whatever the case, you should make sure you understand what is required in order to be within your state's laws as a homeschooler. Almost all fifty states in the United States have truancy laws which require children to be in school after a certain age. Breaking those laws could bring hefty fines or even jail time. Ensuring you follow your state's laws for reporting as a homeschooler might mean the difference between being a home educator and getting entangled with the justice system.

With that said, thanks to my recent move from Washington to California, I have now experienced homeschooling in two different states. There's not much difference between them. Even with different requirements, I am still using the same curriculum and same resources. The only difference is that I keep records in a different way.

In Washington State, where I used to live, we were required to file a Declaration of Intent to homeschool. This is how the state knew the kids weren't truant, but were home with me. We had to teach eleven different subjects, but the law was so open that it didn't specify if you had to teach all eleven subjects every year or just get to them all by the time the kid became an adult. The final requirement was to take a standardized test each year or to have a certified teacher give a thorough evaluation of the child.

In California, where I currently live, the options are a little different. Rather than recognize homeschooling as its own form of education, California offers the option of setting up your own private school and filing your own Private School Affidavit, with the knowledge that you have to follow California's education code. In that case, there are seven subjects to cover and you must keep attendance records. If you don't want to create your own private school, there are numerous options for umbrella schools or homeschool-friendly charter schools you can join.

If you're just starting out and you're not familiar with your local homeschool laws, I highly recommend talking with your local homeschool community or running a Google search for your state's homeschool laws.

Blueprint Sketch #13: Keep it legal.

> Research your state's education laws. What is required of you as a homeschooler? What kinds of records do you need to keep? Do you need to file paperwork with your local school district? If so, when is it due? Do you need to do curriculum or portfolio reviews? Will you have to do standardized testing? What options for testing are available to you as a homeschooler?

Gather all of that paperwork now, and file it in a place where you can find it if you ever need it. If there are certain dates when things are due, put reminders in your calendar now so you don't forget.

Short-term goals

Now that you have a long-term overview of what you hope to accomplish during your child's school years, it's time to focus on this year.

Everything we've done so far has been big. Setting values was like figuring out the location of your house. Defining your preferred methods was similar to deciding whether you were going to have a ranch house, a mobile home, or a hobbit hole. Dreaming about how things might look in the long run was a way of figuring out what you need in your home—how many bedrooms and what kinds of common areas you would need to live comfortably in the way you've imagined.

Now we're going to start narrowing things down until you have a detailed drawing of that home you're building. We're going to focus on the next school year, which will be like choosing your appliances and fixtures. This is the part where you'll decide what subjects you plan to study and decide what curriculum or resources you'll use for the year.

Defining your big picture vision for your child's education should have revealed some subjects or abilities that need specific work. As I write this, I recognize that I can be offering my children much more practice with their communications skills, both written and spoken in groups of people. One of my goals for next year is to find more opportunities for them to be in groups, make presentations, and write in order to communicate their ideas to various groups of people.

Blueprint Sketch #14: What skills need work?

Take five minutes and write a list of the top skills or concepts you want to work on with your child this year. Are there particular subjects they need to work on?

Blueprint Sketch #15: List your ideal extras.

As you looked to the future, were there any subjects that sounded interesting but a little different or outside-the-box? Make a list of all those things you would do if you had enough money, enough time, or the right teacher to help your child learn it.

Write it down even if it sounds a little crazy or out of reach. You never know what opportunities might come up as you're planning. I have a friend whose son wants to go into aeronautics. It sounded odd to her, until she learned of a school where there were high school classes devoted to exactly that: engineering and manufacturing of airplanes.

Setting SMART goals

Before we get too far into choosing curricula, we're going to talk about how to set good goals. You've already looked ahead to the future and imagined your child's ideal education. You've isolated some things you need to work on this year. But before we get ahead of ourselves and start planning ten-hour school days like a Tiger Mom, let's talk about how to set goals.

I first started work on this section on January 6, less than a week after New Year's Day. Two weeks before, all my social media pages were inundated with messages of high hopes. Everyone I knew shared lists of all the wonderful things they'd do in the coming year. They'd lose weight, eat better, live happier, and work harder. But by the time the first week of January had passed, many of those same friends posted messages about burning out and feeling like failures. Why?

New Year's resolutions rarely make good goals.

In the 1960s, organizational psychologist Edwin A. Locke penned his now famous Goal Setting Theory. His theory was that in order for a goal to be effective, it has to be SMART: Specific, Measurable, Achievable, Realistic, and Time-Bound.

Specific Goals

Specific goals give you a very clear idea of what you will be doing. Let's say you're looking into planning a fourth-grade year. You might be tempted to set a goal that says, "Finish 4th grade." That's not very specific. What exactly goes into finishing 4th grade? What subjects are involved? What curriculum/curricula will you use? You might choose one curriculum that encompasses multiple subjects, or you might combine several types of curricula to cover each of your subjects separately.

It's the same with a common New Year's resolution: "Lose Weight." How much weight? How do you plan on losing it? When do you want to lose it by? Why do you want to lose it? Maybe it's not the weight that's the issue, but maybe it's another issue entirely that needs to be dealt with. When we get down to specifics, it's easier to see how to make it to the end of a goal.

In the next section on curricula, we'll be setting specific goals for each subject and identifying the resources needed to complete that goal.

Measurable goals

Making a goal measurable means you can easily decide whether you succeeded or not. A goal that you can measure tells you right away how far you've moved towards reaching that goal.

To use the example of losing weight, making it a measurable goal means adding some numbers to it. "Lose Weight" becomes "lose ten pounds" or "get down to ___ pounds." Now that you have a number attached, you can easily see how close you are to reaching that goal.

When my kids were younger, I had a goal: teach them to read. I think most homeschoolers have this as a goal. After a while, it can become a discouraging goal. For me, I realized that the lofty goal of "reading" was not very helpful in my day-to-day life. It's like setting a goal of "learn math." What exactly did I mean when I thought of reading? There are many different levels of reading ability: recognizing letters; connecting letters with their sounds; putting sounds together; sounding out words; understanding the words; recognizing words without sounding them out; and reading stories and chapter books. The more I looked into the different skills required as part of reading, the more I began to understand that teaching "reading" would be a long process. In order to make that goal measurable, I had to consider the skills my children already had and then decide what the next level of proficiency would look like.

Reading goals you can actually measure might look more like this:

~ be able to sound out three-letter CVC (consonant-vowel-consonant) words like cat, rat, dog, or wig.

~ read aloud all the words in a level 2 reader.

~ read a chapter book alone and be able to retell the basic story later in their own words.

Goals like these are easy to measure. You can tell that the child has reached that level of proficiency when they can do those things. They're also much more specific goals than that nebulous one of "learn how to read."

Achievable goals

My husband and I often joke with our son about the boy winning the Nobel Prize. When he's frustrated with some aspect of school or life and asks why he needs to do it, we'll say, "You need to do this so you can win the Nobel Prize and buy us a hot tub." When he's frustrated with handwriting practice: "When you're a famous scientist, you'll need to be able to report on your findings so you can win the Nobel Prize." When teaching table manners: "This will be useful after you win the Nobel Prize and get to have dinner with the president."

Poor kid. We make sure to tell our son that we're joking about the Nobel Prize. All we really want is the hot tub.

Winning the Nobel Prize is not a goal that I would actually set for anyone. It's a wonderful dream, but it's akin to winning the lottery and a setup for disappointment (just look at poor Tesla, for example). Our true goal is for the boy to be able to communicate his thoughts clearly, both in writing and in speech, which requires practice in various areas that are difficult for him. Winning the Nobel Prize might be great for a bucket list, but it's not something I would consider an achievable goal.

When we talk about achievable goals, it's important to remember how much your children change from year to year and even from month to month. A goal that seemed achievable a few weeks ago might suffer a setback. Likewise, something your child was incapable of last year might be easy to accomplish this year. As parents, we need to adjust our expectations often.

Different children also have different abilities. The goals you set when your oldest was eight years old may not be achievable for your youngest at the same age. On the other hand, your youngest child might have surpassed those goals already and may need further challenges. Try to be flexible when you're setting these goals for your children. This leads to the next part of SMART goals: be realistic.

Realistic goals

I don't know about you, but my life is pretty messy. My home is messy. I don't have a separate room devoted to schooling, so our learning space is spread throughout the house. That means I step on LEGO® bricks in the kitchen, have glitter glued to the dining room table, and have to shuffle piles of laundry in order to make room for us to sit to read.

As much as I wish it did, my life doesn't look like a Pinterest board. I'm pretty sure yours doesn't either. When you set realistic goals, you take into account what your everyday life is like in the house you live in, during the hours you keep, in the community you live in. If you live out in the country, it is not realistic for you to set a goal to visit a science museum once a week—unless you really love driving. If you live in an apartment in the middle of a big city, it's not realistic to set a goal of raising cows and chickens. Back to the goal of losing weight, it's not realistic to set a goal of fitting into a size 6 if you haven't fit in a size 6 since you were 12 years old. Don't make goals that will just set you up for failure and disappointment.

Being realistic about your goals means that you take your real life into account as you plan. Doing so can also set you up to succeed and to feel more content, rather than to continue striving to do something that you're unlikely to accomplish.

Time-bound or time-targeted goals

The last part of SMART goal-setting is time. You can set a goal of losing ten pounds, and never do a thing about it. Or you can sign up and pay for an event like a zombie run or a 5K that's happening in two months, and suddenly, you'll have a lot of motivation to get in better shape.

Time-bound goals mean you have a deadline or a target date to finish or succeed at that goal.

You might know a homeschool family similar to some of the families I know. They are so relaxed that their high schoolers don't have their school work done before graduation time. They have celebration parties like everyone else, but then the truth comes out: the homeschooler still has three or four subjects to finish. So they spend the summer, next fall, and the following winter moseying through their subjects without any strict deadline about getting it done. They already missed any deadlines for college admission, and they already "walked" and celebrated with all their friends so there's no real motivation to finish the work.

Other families I know spend their summers "just finishing up" and then wonder why they don't feel excited for a new school year in the fall. If you school year-round by choice, this looks a little different. You're either happy with the progress you're making, or you feel perpetually behind.

If you have college-bound children, time-bound goals become extremely clear right around junior year. Suddenly, there are a lot of things that need to be done in a short period of time. There are standardized tests to take, transcripts to prepare, applications to fill out, essays to write, and financial aid to apply for. All of these tasks have strict deadlines. If you miss them, you have to wait six or twelve months to try again.

Elementary goals usually aren't quite so dire. But if you find yourself always behind and trying to catch up, it may be useful to examine your goals and double-check how you're managing the time involved. In the next section, I'll show you how to break down your goals and your curriculum so you can better visualize how things will go. We'll also set some minimum goals that will make this easier when life gets too complex.

On a side note, missing a time-based goal might also mean that the goal is unrealistic or simply unachievable. You may set a goal of teaching your child to read by the time she turns five, but she might not have the ability to do so. Your goal might be to get through a level of math curriculum, but you find that your child needs more practice with multiplication tables before moving on to long division. Try to be flexible here, but not so nonchalant that time just flies by without anything happening.

Yearly goals

Now that you know how to set better goals, it's time to set some for your coming year.

Considering all the things you've learned already, what specific things would you like to cover in your homeschool this year?

Knowing where your children are academically, socially, emotionally, physically, and possibly even spiritually, what are the areas where you would like to see improvement this year? You may want to wimp out and simply write "Survive the year" as your goal. I usually flail a bit on this one, too. But with a little extra effort, I'm sure you'll be able to think of two or three goals for each child that will help guide your year.

Blueprint Sketch #16: Set your yearly goals.

> What are two or three areas you would like to help your child improve on this year? What are some special skills or abilities you would like your child to learn? Write down any ideas you have.
>
> Now, take each of those ideas and break it down into parts to make specific, measurable, achievable, realistic, and time-sensitive goals. The time part is already done for you, if you're operating on your school year.

Here's how this process might look. I would like for my son to be able to give reports to groups of people. I write down an idea like this: "Have the kid give a report."

It's a good idea to start with, but I need to break it down in order to make it a goal. What kinds of things go into giving a report? I need to teach him how to organize his thoughts, how to choose what to report on, how to outline his idea, and how to give a speech and get over the nerves of being in front of a crowd. Then, I need to have him give that report in front of family, then friends, then a larger group in order to gain more experience and confidence.

Now I have enough details to be able to make this a goal and add it to my homeschool plans. Instead of some nebulous goal of giving a report, I have a clearer idea how much work will go into it. I can also start gathering family and friends to become the audience, which means setting a date for the report. I might even see if other homeschoolers might want to make a special co-op event out of it. Now we have a deadline to prepare for. That idea turned into a specific, measurable, achievable, realistic, and time-bound goal.

Need another example? My daughter, the art lover, would like to show off her art. The hard part is deciding what pieces to display and how to prepare them for an audience to enjoy. One of the things I would like to help her with this year is how to prepare her best work and put the final touches on it. In order to make it a time-bound goal, I need to find an art show for her to participate in or put one together for her. Once that is set, it's time to help her prepare her pieces, take the time to make them as good as possible, and learn to frame or display them so people can enjoy them. Ultimately, this process can help her in preparing a future portfolio as well.

For some of your ideas, you might decide that the goal portion is solved by simply finding a class or special program that the child can attend. In those cases, the teacher or mentor is the one responsible for those nitpicky details and you just have to help by following through. This can be very beneficial as well.

Many of my goals might be outside of the usual reading, writing, and arithmetic I have to teach, but they are particular things I want the kids to learn and experience. In a way, my goals reflect a desire to help the kids communicate what they've learned in order to help others. Your goals might be about your children building strong character, or learning to make friends, or becoming disciplined in order to finish school work.

I know there are a few of you out there who are already thinking this is way too complicated. It doesn't have to be. Let's break it down in a different way.

Subject goals

One of the easiest ways for me to plan a school year is to look at the subjects I should be teaching. These are common just about everywhere. Start with "the Three R's" and go from there.

Blueprint Sketch #17: List your subjects.

What subjects would you like to cover this year? Make a list of them. My yearly list always includes math, science, history, reading, writing, language mechanics like spelling and grammar, and fine art. This year, I'll also include Latin, Spanish, world geography, health and physical education, and computer use. Depending on your values, you might also include Bible study, character studies, music, occupational education, economics, or any other number of subjects.

Blueprint Sketch #18: List your extracurricular activities.

Don't forget the sports! Now list all of those "extra" activities you forgot under the subject list. This is where you list all the sports, clubs, dance, music, art, theater, and church events you'll be attending during the year. Are there any particular activities you'd like to get your child involved in, even if you don't know where or how yet? Many places will have special deals around the start of the school year, so it's easy to enroll in a new Taekwondo, ballet, or gymnastics class if you're thinking about trying it. If your child wants to do baseball or football or soccer, now is a good time to check out where the local teams and leagues are and how you can get involved.

Blueprint Sketch #19: Write a subject overview.

For each subject and activity you want your child to learn this year, write a short note about your plans for that subject. This might mean working through a particular textbook you already have in mind, or it might mean enrolling in a class. You might make a note about your child's proficiency if it's a subject like reading, or you might note that you want your child to practice a skill three times a week.

For example, here is part of my list for my daughter's upcoming year.

~ Math—Khan Academy; finish 4th grade. Life of Fred lessons 4 days a week.

~ Reading—half an hour daily reading

~ Writing—journal writing twice a week, narration for subject notebooks.

~ Latin—one root word per week, *Getting Started with Latin* lesson 3 times a week.

~ Science—Biology, twice a week. Cell models, biome projects, and human anatomy.

~ History—the Ancients, from pre-history to the Fall of Rome.

~ Gymnastics—find local class?

This is just the start of it. Are those goals specific? Some of them are. For others, I still need to come up with a few more details before I can do anything about them.

Why aren't we choosing curricula first, and then basing our goals on that? This part requires a little finesse, as we'll be doing a little of both. If you've already chosen your curricula based on the values and methods we talked about in earlier sections, then this goal-setting part could be easy for you. If you still haven't picked out curricula or you're not sure how you want to teach certain subjects, then setting goals might help you choose.

For instance, if you want to teach spelling but don't know where to start, you can think through your goals for spelling. Do you want your child to learn spelling in a multi-sensory way? Then you'll want a curriculum that does that, like All About Spelling. Do you want your child to go through leveled spelling lists? Then you'll want to find a set of grade-appropriate lists that you can work through. Do you want your child to learn to spell by daily practice with groups of words that use similar patterns? Then you'll want a curriculum like Sequential Spelling. Maybe as you think through it, you'll discover that you don't actually need a separate spelling curriculum because you can teach it through your other grammar or language arts course work.

By the time you're done with this, you might notice that you have a ridiculous number of things you want to cover. If you only have three or four things listed, I admire your restraint. Every year when I get to the end of this list, I feel overwhelmed. I usually have multiple foreign languages, martial arts, chess clubs, art shows, park and museum days, and all the regular academic subjects for a standard school year. How will I ever manage it all?

Reality check: it's possible that you won't. That's why we're doing this now, before you're drowning in all these great ideas and have turned into an anxious mess.

Reality check

Does this sound familiar? You started homeschooling in the fall with all the fervor of a forest fire in a drought, but by the middle of February you've taken to writing sarcastic comments on your friends' Facebook posts about how you were meant to be an unschooler and you can't remember the last time you changed out of pajamas.

Most homeschoolers are no strangers to burnout. We try to hide it, usually because we're afraid of people seeing us not doing enough. We don't want people to know that homeschooling is actually really hard sometimes, so we put on a happy face and put up another cute art project on Facebook or Pinterest and talk about how much we love it. We're not doing anyone any favors that way. Pushing harder at more things is the quickest way I know for a homeschool parent to end up throwing in the towel.

Want to give yourself a sure recipe for burnout? Try this:

1. Enroll your child in every extracurricular activity and free class available. You're not a real homeschooler if you're not taking part in gymnastics, swimming lessons, art lessons, chess club, and private music lessons for piano, guitar, violin, and harp. If there isn't already a basketball or soccer league you can join, you need to organize one and coach it. If a local museum is giving a free presentation, you need to be there. Make sure you do all the local parks & recreation classes on Saturdays, too.

2. Use every curriculum labeled by someone as "the best." The best curriculum requires an hour of watching a video, a hands-on project, a worksheet, and a test for each school day. Make sure you combine at least six of these each and every day, or it doesn't count.

3. Spend any free time you have reading homeschool blogs and looking at pretty crafts and projects on Pinterest. Make sure you follow people with large houses, large yards, or large school rooms. Make sure to compare your own home and family with their lovely, clean pictures. If you don't feel guilty or jealous, you're following the wrong families.

Try a little harder to find homeschoolers who are doing everything right and keeping everything clean while running family farms, writing daily blogs with photos, and making every food item from scratch.

I'm only being a little facetious here. I am constantly talking with homeschool parents who are doing exactly those things and wondering why they are so tired or so discouraged. I've been there, too. My husband talks me down from an "I'm not doing enough compared to _____" fit at least three times a year.

You will probably suffer some burnout along the way, if you haven't already. I hope this planning will help prevent you from getting there. Be honest when you're there. It will help the other homeschoolers in your community see your reality and not the show. In my experience, whenever a fellow homeschooler admits to burnout, the whole community rallies to help encourage him or her to rest and recover. You might be surprised to learn how many of the others around you, especially the ones who look like they have it all together, deal with burnout and feelings of insecurity about their role as homeschool parents.

Why am I talking about burnout right in the middle of a chapter about setting goals? Because I know you. You're optimistic. You're a homeschool version of a Tiger Mom. You're going to do it perfectly on your first try and no one will ever be able to criticize your ability to educate your own children at home. You have a lot to prove. Maybe you have parents who aren't convinced about homeschooling. Maybe you have a spouse who sometimes expresses a wish for you to get a job so you can send the kids to a nice private school instead. Maybe you have a friend who constantly quizzes you or your children about their knowledge to see if you measure up to their standards. Maybe you have kids who wonder why they don't get a shiny new backpack and a 7 a.m. bus ride like the other kids.

I know. It's a lot of pressure. That's why we have to be realistic about it. I hope that setting your values in the first section helped ease some of the tension you get from the judgment of others. But you still have to deal with judgment from yourself. And that's why we need to make sure you set realistic goals.

Keeping your spouse or close family in the loop can also be of benefit during these times. My husband may not plan curriculum or read the same resources I do, but he shares my values and he can see when I've taken on too much. He often helps me navigate the more difficult periods of homeschooling by talking through it with me and reminding me of the things that are most important.

Weekly goals

Now that we've had our little chat about burnout, it's time to keep working on our goals. For anyone who might have trouble narrowing down all their choices, the following exercises can be very helpful. By the end of this, you'll have each of your days planned out and will be able to see where you need to make adjustments.

Blueprint Sketch #20: How often will we study each subject?

Take out your list of all the subjects and activities you plan to do this year. Beside each subject, write the number of days you plan to work on that topic each week. Will it require daily practice? Twice a week? Three times a week? Only once a week? Just write down a little number. Also, put a little star next to any subject that you consider a high priority—a subject or activity that you won't drop, no matter what.

Now that you know how often you'll work on each subject, we're going to put each of those subjects on a daily list.

Blueprint Sketch #21: These are the days of the week.

Take out five sheets of scratch paper, one for each school day in a week. If you plan to do school only four days a week, then get out four pieces of paper. If you plan to do school seven days a week, then I think you're a little crazy, but you'll need seven sheets of paper. At the top of the pages, write the days of the week.

Now, write each of your subjects on the day of the week that you plan to teach it.

First, for every subject that needs daily practice, write it on each page. If you plan to do math every day, write it on every page. If your child needs to practice something every day, like a musical instrument or a sport, put it on the days now. Yes, this seems excessive, but writing it on every page will give you a much better visual of those things actually taking up time in your school day.

Do you need to do this for every child? It's up to you. This is the point at which I usually decide to combine my kids in as many subjects as possible, because I realize I cannot teach customized curricula from six or seven different subjects to each of them every single day. However, if each of your children will be doing very different things, you might want to do this for each of them.

Now, for each subject you plan to teach three days a week, write it on three of the days. I usually do Monday, Wednesday, and Friday, since that makes it easy.

For every subject you plan to teach twice a week, pick the days for each of them. I find that it helps to stagger your subjects. I like to teach history twice a week and science twice a week, but it would make for a very full day if I did them both on the same day. I choose to do history on Mondays and Thursdays, and science on Tuesdays and Fridays.

For anything you'll do once a week, pick a day for it and write it in there.

At this point, each of your days is probably pretty full. Did you make sure to put all your sports practices and club days on there, too?

You might be in one of several emotional states at this moment. You might be overwhelmed by the huge number of things you think you're going to do every day. You might be underwhelmed because it doesn't look like much. Or you might think everything looks just right. Before we move on, let's make sure what you're planning will actually work.

Blueprint Sketch #22: Is this SMART?

> For each activity listed, how long will it take? Write a rough estimate next to each subject on your daily lists.

As a rough estimate, I give myself an hour for each subject. Now, I know in my heart that my kids can finish their math for the day in fifteen minutes if it's a perfect day. If everyone got enough sleep and the sun is shining and there are pigs flying in the sky, we'll be done in fifteen minutes or less. But I plan for it to take an hour.

I have another subject I teach called Getting Started with Latin, and each lesson is very short. Since I teach it and we all do it out loud together, I know we can be done in ten minutes or less. It's easy for me to schedule that one four days a week, because it doesn't require much time.

Art projects usually take about two hours from start to finish, as long as I have everything prepped and ready beforehand, which is why I put art on a day that doesn't have a lot of other time-intensive projects.

About how long will your subjects take each day? Add them all together and figure out how much time you're planning to school on each day. Is that amount of time realistic for the age and abilities of your child? If you add in extra time for breaks, meals, and life as a family, will this schedule be manageable for you? Will this schedule allow you, the homeschooling parent, to be a human person with interests and hobbies other than the education of your children?

If you have ten hours of school planned for your kindergartner, I'm here to say that you sound like many of the beginning homeschoolers I've met (I was this way in the beginning, too). Don't worry! You have plenty of time to cover all those wonderful things you want to teach. For now, let's focus on the most important things.

Blueprint Sketch #23: Make adjustments.

For every day that you have too many things planned, can you combine subjects? For instance, if you want to do handwriting, spelling, and grammar on the same day, you can do all three in one language arts exercise. You can combine history with social studies and geography by studying the places and people along with the historical events.

If you can't combine subjects, are there any you can cut out? This is always hard. There are so many wonderful learning opportunities available, but no one can do all of them. Try to focus on the most important things. What things could you cut out or give up to make a more manageable and realistic schedule?

Another thing to consider is how energetic your child is. If your child has an outside class in the afternoon that will require a lot of energy, do you want them to put in a full day of intense school before that, or do you want to make sure they have plenty of time to take a break before the next thing? If your child is the type to need a lot of exercise and plenty of wiggle breaks, you'll want to take that into account as well.

Also consider your own needs as the teacher/parent/keeper of the home here. If you're managing a very full school day with multiple kids, keeping a house clean, cooking meals, caring for pets, and maintaining a garden, will you have a single moment to read a book or draw a picture just for the sheer pleasure of doing something for yourself? When will you run errands? When will you sleep?

Adjust each of your daily lists to make them more manageable. They might still be pretty full, or you might have a day or two with only a few subjects listed to give yourself and your family some time to play together. We're going to do one last project with these lists, and then we'll move on to the great hunt for curricula and books.

Setting minimums

At some point in your homeschooling career, your plans will be disrupted. I don't know a single family that hasn't had to deal with illnesses, especially during rough flu seasons. There are others who have had to go through very hard times: death in the family, diagnosis with a chronic illness, hospitalizations, or natural disasters. On the less scary but equally difficult side, many homeschoolers have welcomed new babies to the family, have dealt with a move to a new town or country, or have taken the opportunity to travel for an extended period of time.

What do you do when something changes your plans and you can't put in a full school day like you've scheduled? I hope nothing scary will happen in your family, but having a plan in place can be incredibly helpful.

We're going to set these plans with the hope that you will never have to fall back to them. I call them my "bare minimums"—the things that need to be done in order to mark off a school day, even if we don't do everything I have planned. To be honest, I fall back on my bare minimum plans for at least a week or two every year. If it's not the flu or a cross-country move, it's usually a slight case of burnout that needs to be treated with more afternoon naps and fewer tears during history lessons.

My bare minimums are reading, language arts, and math. If my kids read part of any book, it counts. If they do any sort of communication in writing or speech, either creative or non-fiction, we're good. And if they do any sort of math, from counting coins to algebraic equations, I'm counting it.

When we were in the middle of our cross-country move a few months ago, my kids had to do three sections in Khan Academy, one page from Daily Language Review (which covers language mechanics), and half an hour of reading each day. We finished our school year with only those three requirements, but you can imagine they also learned a lot during the move. They learned about new cultures, about different biomes and plant life, about state laws, and about navigating with maps. They also learned what to do when you blow a tire in the middle of central California on a very hot day. That situation taught us that when the zombie apocalypse comes, we want a tow truck driver on our team.

Speaking of the zombie apocalypse, let's put this question in a fun way. If the zombie apocalypse came right in the middle of your next school year, what would you continue to teach and why?

Would you drop everything and unschool? This is the choice for many, and it's not a bad choice at all. I think sometimes homeschool parents don't see how much their kids are learning until after the event. A few years ago, we traveled several hundred miles to the funeral of my husband's grandfather. Because it was very sudden and we weren't sure where we would be staying or how things would go, I let school go for a few weeks. I was glad I did. There was grief to be felt, family to be comforted, a grandfather to be remembered, and belongings to be reminisced over. Those things were far more important at that time than finding the y-intercept from an algebraic equation.

I have a dear friend who cared for her father during his last year of life. It was incredibly difficult for her as she was in and out of hospital visits and dealing with the emotions involved with the inevitable loss. She homeschooled her children during this time. They often carried their backpacks full of schoolwork from one place to another. When she first told me about that year, she thought she had failed as a homeschooler because she hadn't done enough during that time.

Several years later, she came to understand how much her kids had really learned during that year. It's not something you could take a test on, but it's something that gave her kids more humanity and better emotional intelligence because they walked through it with her. It was a valuable, albeit painful and difficult, experience. They definitely received a priceless year of education, with or without the school books.

Try to think through this now, so when the time comes you don't have to deal with the burden of guilt on top of whatever difficult thing is happening. If you would honestly decide to unschool during an event and allow your children to learn from the event itself rather than stricter forms of education, then stick to it. Don't feel bad when that time comes and you fall back on a more relaxed style. If there are two or three subjects that you deem the most important things, then stick to those and let all those Pinterest projects go hang when the time comes.

Blueprint Sketch #24: Set your bare minimums.

In your opinion, what are the main things that need to happen in order for you to mark a school day done? If worse came to worst, what would you still hope to teach or impart to your children? What counts as education when time, energy, or health is limited?

Set your bare minimums now. Put them in writing. Use this wording: "I would like to complete a number of subjects this year, but if anything happens, we will do _____ and it will be enough."

Goals review

Part of having manageable plans is knowing what your goals are. It's hard to have realistic expectations about homeschooling if you don't have an end result in mind. In this section, we've worked our way from the big picture of a future adulthood down to a list of things that could be worked on this year. You learned more about setting goals you can actually accomplish, by making them specific, measurable, achievable, reasonable, and time-targeted. You set your sights high and listed all the things you want to work on, then made a short list of bare minimums that you can do when life gets hard.

Here are those steps, one more time.

~ For each of your children, take some time to think about what adulthood might look like for them. What does your child want to be when he grows up? What are the things he is most interested in?

~ What are your child's strengths and weaknesses? What skills do they have that will help them do well in adulthood? What skills need work?

~ What kind of an adult do you hope your child will grow up to be? What traits are important to you that you can focus on now?

~ Do you hope your child might attend college? What kind of education might your child need in order to meet their future goals as an adult?

~ What can you do to help your child succeed in the next ten years? Five years? This year?

~ What school subjects do you want to cover this year, either because of requirements or because of your future goals? What do you hope your child will learn from each subject?

~ What will each of your school days look like with all your subjects and extracurricular activities written in? Are there any things you need to cut or combine before moving on?

~ If anything should happen to disrupt your normal homeschool life, what are your minimum requirements for getting through a school day? Are there certain subjects that absolutely must be done? Will you choose to unschool and trust that learning is still happening during that time?

Part Four: Curriculum

Choose your curriculum

Now that you have your values set, you have a better idea of what your methods look like, and you have a basic image in your mind about your goals and subject choices for this year, it's time to pick your curriculum. If we continue the analogy of building a house, choosing your curriculum is similar to choosing your paint colors. How will you decorate each room in your house? Will you use wallpaper, paint a mural, or use textured paints to create the right mood? What materials will you use to help you teach the subjects you want to teach this year?

If you've been homeschooling for any amount of time, you probably know how difficult it can be to choose curricula. There are so many options available, and some of them can be quite expensive. If you ask for recommendations, you get half a dozen different answers and everyone swears that their program is the best thing ever. How do you ever choose? This is where I hope all that work on values and methods will pay off for you.

So where do you start?

First, let's take an inventory of all the things you already have. Then, we'll see where there are gaps and start deciding what you need to buy or to create for yourself. I'll try to show you as many different options as I can to help you search for the right supplies for you.

Blueprint Sketch #25: Check your inventory.

Look at the lists you made in the yearly goals and subject goals sections. For each subject you plan to teach, note which ones you already have curriculum or supplies for. Start gathering these resources in one place in your house: a bookshelf, a free corner, or a tote bag. We'll need them for the next section.

Blueprint Sketch #26: Start a shopping list.

For some subjects, you might know what you want but don't own it yet. Start a shopping list. Depending on how crazy you are about finding good deals, you might want to keep this list in your purse or wallet or near your computer. It will help you know what to look for when you're at used curricula sales, garage sales, conventions, or when your favorite website emails you about a sale.

Make a note on your subject list that you'll be using a particular book or curriculum. We'll need to start looking for things you haven't decided on yet.

If you're going with a unit study format, each of your units will cover those subjects you want to teach. In this case, rather than choosing a curriculum for each subject, you'll want to choose which units you want to do during the year and decide whether you have the supplies required for each of those units. You'll also want to make a note of any subjects that will not be covered in your unit studies for some reason.

For everything else, we're going to start a treasure hunt. You'll either find what you're looking for or decide, like I often do, to put it together yourself. I'll show you my best techniques for searching, list some of my favorite places to purchase from, and then walk you through how to create your own curricula.

Boxed curricula

One of the easiest ways to finish planning a homeschool year is to purchase a boxed curriculum, also called school-in-a-box. A boxed curriculum provides everything you need—all the books, the schedules, the lesson plans, the review sheets and tests, manipulatives, and any other instructional materials you need—in a box (or two or three). Many parents swear by their choice of boxed curriculum provider. It's easy, since everything is done for you. All you have to do is facilitate the daily lesson plans that are already provided.

Many of the homeschool catalog companies are now providing full boxed curriculum plans, since it makes shopping so easy. Every one of these is quite different. The third-grade box from Sonlight would have only a few similar items to the third-grade box from Timberdoodle, for instance.

A quick Google search revealed that there are dozens of homeschool companies now providing boxed curriculum. Depending on your preferences, you could go with Sonlight, Heart of Dakota, A Beka, My Father's World, Veritas Press, Calvert, Oak Meadow, or the sets from Timberdoodle or Rainbow Resource. There are many, many more.

If you plan to purchase a boxed curriculum, the good news is that you're almost done choosing curricula. Congratulations! Don't skip ahead just yet, though. You'll want to make sure you're not missing anything. Some boxed curricula don't include math or science programs, so you need to double-check if you have those. Others are science-heavy and don't include much in the way of language arts. After you decide which one you're using, see if there is anything missing from your yearly goals.

I love boxed curricula. I sometimes dream of having all those books delivered to my home in one huge batch, and having a chart that tells me what to do, how to do it, and when to get it done. In reality, my values don't allow me to buy them, so I have to make those wonderful plans for myself. I like interest-led, individualized education too much to buy something someone else planned for me. I also lack the space and funds required to purchase every material we'll use in a year. I use library resources as often as I can.

If you choose not to use a ready-made curriculum, then your next step is to find out exactly what you'll need to put together to prepare your homeschool year. Many homeschool parents do it this way.

Blueprint Sketch #27: Choose your boxed curriculum.

> Do you plan to use a boxed curriculum? If so, purchase it now or put it on a wish list so you can keep an eye out for sales. You'll need to look into what subjects will be covered by your curriculum. Is anything missing that you need to plan for? Does it include art appreciation or music? Will you do a foreign language? What will you do for math or science?

Where to find curricula

If you aren't using a boxed curriculum, or you need to find a curriculum for an extra subject, it's time to make some choices. Choosing curricula for each of your subjects can require a bit of finesse and some good google fu skills. Here are the best ways I know of to find curricula, starting with my favorite.

1. Visit a used curriculum sale hosted by a local homeschool group.

I was lucky when I first started homeschooling. A local friend served as my mentor for the first few years, giving me her used curricula and talking me through the myriad of emotions that go along with the decision to homeschool. She also took me to my first used curriculum sale, hosted by a somewhat local homeschool co-op. Before that point, I had only heard rumors of the many types of curricula available. At that sale, I was able to look at many different types of curricula and talk to veteran homeschool parents about what they liked and disliked about them. I fondly call those sales "Curriculum Petting Zoos."

If you are a veteran homeschool parent, I encourage you to invite a new homeschooler to your favorite used curriculum sale. If you don't know of any sales, ask around the local homeschool groups, or consider organizing your own. They're a great way to get homeschoolers together to share ideas and resources, not to mention a great way to earn some cash on supplies you won't need anymore.

2. Ask a local homeschool group.

If you have park days or field trips, ask the other homeschoolers there what they use. I've had many different conversations at local co-op events about curricula, usually started by someone saying, "I need to teach _____. What do you use?" You'll probably hear half a dozen different suggestions and methods, but you might find something you'll want to learn more about. Depending on how much you want to know, or what other people have, you might be able to borrow or look at particular curricula you're interested in.

If you don't already belong to a local homeschool community, I highly encourage you to find one. Depending on where you live, there might already be groups you can join full of homeschool parents that are similar to you and have children of similar ages. Many of them have websites or groups on Facebook or Yahoo where they communicate about upcoming events and opportunities. Not all groups charge a fee for membership. Some groups are more relaxed than others and might have regular get-togethers for fun and socializing. Other groups have organized classes that your children can enroll in. Being part of a community can provide a source of great encouragement and a place to share ideas and resources.

If you don't have a homeschool community, or you don't wish to be part of the one that currently exists in your area, consider starting your own. There is probably another homeschool parent in the area wishing for the same kind of group you want. Once you meet up together, you can organize planning days or curriculum swaps.

Local charter or umbrella schools might have good information about homeschool curricula, too, especially if it's a charter that a lot of homeschoolers frequent. You might disagree about whether using a charter school is technically homeschooling, but that's a subject for another day. When you're searching for curricula, you just need people to talk to who understand your particular educational needs.

3. Visit a homeschool convention.

If you want to get an idea of what is available and meet some of the people behind certain curriculum types, spend a day or two at one of the homeschool conventions in your state. It might require a bit of travel, but if you go with other homeschool friends, you can share the expense (as well as the fun).

At a convention, you'll be able to see setups from and purchase many of the items from the different catalog companies as well as curriculum writers and providers. You can look through all the different types of curricula and browse the books and games and puzzles and manipulatives available. The only difference between this and a used curriculum sale is the price. Buying new at a convention might not fit your budget, but if it does, this is a great way to get what you want.

4. Ask online.

There are hundreds, if not thousands, of online groups and forums devoted to homeschooling. Every year during the fall, there are posts by new homeschoolers asking about curricula and how to teach different subjects. Join one of those forums, read the posts made by others, and see what kinds of things you might want to use. Some of the most active forums I know of are at homeschool.com, secularhomeschool.com, and forums.welltrainedmind.com. I've belonged to the last one for over four years and have found a lot of great resources there. Before I joined a local homeschool community, the online forums served as a lifeline to me and helped me connect to other homeschoolers going through the same things I was.

One of the benefits of asking in an online forum is that you can have a conversation about what you want, and others can make recommendations and compare and contrast their experiences. You can also ask more questions about anything that is mentioned. Often, parents who help with curriculum choices will list everything they use for a certain year to give you an idea of their style. This can be hugely beneficial if you're just starting out and have no idea where to begin looking. You might ask about math curricula and end up with a long list of recommendations for every other subject under the sun, too.

You can often find curricula resale groups that are connected to online groups and forums, too. Take advantage of the significant discounts you can get by buying your curricula used.

5. Read Cathy Duffy's *101 Top Picks for Homeschool Curriculum*.

Cathy Duffy has been reviewing homeschool curricula for thirty years. One of the things I like about her book, especially for new homeschoolers, is that she asks all those questions about your teaching and learning preferences and then recommends resources categorically for the different educational philosophies. Her book includes only her top recommendations for resources, so you won't get any extras here, and often the best curricula can be the most expensive.

If you want an idea about everything that's available, the website at cathyduffyreviews.com has links to reviews for almost any imaginable resource. It's not listed by teaching or learning style, unfortunately, but it is still nice if you want to look for more information about anything that is recommended to you.

6. Read catalogs.

I may be a little abnormal, but I go crazy for homeschool and teacher catalogs. Sometime in July, I start getting stacks of catalogs in my mailbox from different providers. The Rainbow Resource catalog is by far my favorite, with over a thousand pages of products that are personally reviewed by the staff. I lug that thing to the park and the beach every summer and highlight things I want to look into or purchase. When I need games and manipulatives, I look at Timberdoodle's catalog first, and most of my science supplies come from Home Science Tools. When I'm looking for good literature for upcoming studies, I like to browse the Sonlight catalog, or the catalogs from Veritas Press, Beautiful Feet Books, or Classical Conversations.

There are many catalogs available, and they often contain good information about and reviews of each product.

Some of my favorite teacher catalogs are those from Evan-Moor and Learning Resources. I can get a lot of ideas from those catalogs, and often use resources from curriculum providers like Evan-Moor and Scholastic during my school years. The only difference between homeschool catalogs and teaching catalogs is that the homeschool catalogs usually cater to the particular needs of homeschoolers rather than to the needs of a teacher in a large classroom setting. Teaching catalogs often contain products for classroom management and decoration that I have no use for. The curriculum is often written for classroom settings and large groups as well, and may need to be adapted if you're using it for only one or two children.

Still, looking through catalogs can be a great way to familiarize yourself with the many options available and help you narrow down your own choices.

7. Run a Google search.

I love the Internet. I am so glad I live in the current day and age, when everything I ever wanted to know (and didn't want to know) is available with a few keystrokes.

When in doubt, Google it. This should probably be much higher on this list, except that I find great value in the experiences of others when it comes to curriculum. If you don't have a local group to chat with, or you're just not finding what you want, run a Google search.

If you aren't a confident Internet researcher, let me give you a few tips. First of all, make sure you use several different search terms together to narrow down your results. You don't want to do a search for "spelling" or you'll get too many results that have nothing to do with what you're looking for. I recommend adding the word "homeschool" to anything you search for, and possibly the word "curriculum" for good measure. Running a search for "homeschool spelling curriculum" will get you several review sites, as well as a few spelling curricula providers, like All About Spelling and Sequential Spelling.

Depending on your preferences, you might want to try some different search terms when searching for science curricula. Science can be a polarizing subject. Depending on where you are on the spectrum of origins, you'll have to be clever to find what you need for science. If you want creation-based science, you can use search terms like "faith-based," "creation," or "Christian" to narrow down your choices. If you want evolutionary science in particular, you can add terms like "secular" or "non-Christian." It seems to me that many of the curricula written for homeschool science tend to be overtly Christian and creation-based, but you might have the opposite impression. Either way, I find that curriculum writers spend a lot of energy trying to prove or disprove a side rather than devoting themselves to the type of science projects an elementary-grade child might be interested in. If you're looking for a curriculum that doesn't have a dog in the fight either way, you'll need to do some serious hunting. My best bet has been to find one or two book publishers I know and like and purchase most of my products from them.

8. Visit a local teachers' supply store.

Depending on your needs as a homeschool parent, you might be able to find many of the things you need at your local teachers' supply store. I get many great ideas by wandering around and looking at the items in those stores, and it also gives me a renewed sense of gratitude that I don't have to teach in a large classroom full of kids.

Teachers' supply stores will have all of your traditional subjects from the publishers that teachers use in schools. Evan-Moor and Scholastic will be a common sight. I use and enjoy many different books by Evan-Moor and Scholastic, so that's not a bad thing. However, if you're looking for Apologia Science or Sequential Spelling or the Life of Fred series, you're most likely going to strike out here.

9. Build your own.

If you're like me, and you have a particular idea about how you want to teach a particular subject, you might do all of the above things and still not find what you're looking for. Or maybe you found something you like but it's too far out of your price range. In that case, it might be time to branch out and do it yourself.

Blueprint Sketch #28: Find your curricula.

> This might be the most time-consuming step of this whole process. Choose curricula for any subjects you plan to work on this year. If you're going to do unit studies, choose which studies you'll work on. If you don't plan to use a pre-written curriculum, decide what you will use. At this point, purchase any books or textbooks you're going to use or borrow them from the library so you can make more detailed plans for your calendar.

You don't need all your supplies or supplementary books yet, just the main textbooks, encyclopedias, or teaching books you'll be using for your core subjects. For the calendar portion, we'll need to know how many pages you'll be covering of each thing so we can set some weekly and daily goals.

Do-It-Yourself curriculum overview

I'm not picky so much as I am stubborn. When I first started out, I took umbrage at all those textbooks that told me how to do things. "Say this." "Teach that." "Give that test." I know that some people thrive on this type of curriculum (and to be honest, I'm a little jealous of you if you do). I don't. For several years, I've struggled to find the right curricula for my needs. Anything I do buy ends up being modified almost beyond recognition. I'm that recipe reviewer on allrecipes.com who says, "I made this, but I was out of garlic powder so I substituted coriander. It added great flavor! I also don't like soy sauce, so I put in some chicken stock. I didn't want to bake it in the oven because it was too hot that day. I put it in a pan on the stove on medium heat and covered it. Worked great. Five stars!"

Because I have to do things in my own way, I developed a system for building my own book lists and project ideas for my school year. I like to plan an entire year at once, since I can connect subjects to each other, plan around my holidays, and get a sense of where we'll be going in various subjects during the year.

I've adopted a thirty-six-week system for my schooling. There are several reasons for this. First of all, 36 weeks of school, done 5 days a week, is the equivalent of the 180-day school year required by school districts in several states. Your state might have different requirements for attendance and record-keeping, but for me, that number seemed as good as any. Another reason I like the thirty-six-week system is that it gives me an ability to break things up. If you told me I had to plan 180 individual school days, I would probably laugh hysterically in your face before dousing myself in alcohol and lighting myself on fire. Planning that intensely on that large of a level is too much for a normal person to handle (kudos if you manage it). When I cut it down to planning thirty-six weeks of school, it seems much more manageable. If thirty-six weeks still sounds crazy, imagine dividing that into six terms of six weeks each, or four quarters of just nine weeks. Now we're getting into normal people territory.

In this section, I'll show you how I put together my own topics and book lists, using mostly free library resources. The process consists of nine steps that coincide with most of what we've done so far, and will be very similar to the way we'll break up the pre-written curricula you already have.

DIY Curriculum Step #1: Choose what to teach and how to teach it.

We already did a lot of subject listing during the goals section. If you have several subjects for which you have no curriculum, you might want to combine them all in a series of short unit studies. If at all possible, consider basing the majority of your teaching round a single subject. When everything is tied to one subject, it won't feel quite so disjointed, and you can reinforce your teaching across all subjects.

There are a few different ways to do this. One of my friends picks a common theme for her year, then builds her curriculum around that. She is working through the fifty states of the U.S. right now, creating unit studies out of picture books that highlight life in different states and regions. Our methods look different, but our planning process is nearly identical. In fact, we often look over each other's plans to exchange new ideas.

I like putting things in order chronologically, so I tie the majority of my school subjects into chronological world history. I can cover just about everything this way, including geography, social science, reading, writing, and art. If I got really into it, I could even include science and scientific advances as a tie-in from history studies.

Science is a subject that generally stands alone for me. Doing it yourself can require a lot of planning, but I'll show you some of the ways I put my plans together. I can usually add art and writing to our study of science, as well as presentation and communication skills.

If you're doing something like a musician or artist study, it can be helpful to put together your list ahead of time so you know what needs to be gathered for each week.

You'll also want to decide how you'll be teaching the subject. Do you want to do hands-on projects? Do you want to read a piece of text and then have worksheets or notebooking pages to review what was read? Do you want to check out picture books on the subjects and use those to learn about the subjects you're studying? Do you want to watch videos? I use all of those methods for my subjects, but I generally lean more heavily toward one or another for certain things. I use a lot of videos and hands-on experiments for science, but tend toward using encyclopedias, picture books, and source text for history.

What subjects do you want to create plans for? What kinds of materials do you hope to use to teach each of those subjects?

DIY Curriculum Step #2: Find your spine.

Unless you are brilliant or you have a doctorate in the subject you plan to teach, the odds are that you don't know everything about the subject you're planning for. Even if you have no idea where to begin or what to cover, don't worry. Overviews are very easy to find, in the form of spines.

What is a spine? The term spine is used to describe a book or list that serves as the backbone of a curriculum or course of study. Homeschoolers use this term to talk about the main book, textbook, or encyclopedia they use for their studies on a particular subject. It forms the basic skeletal structure for your other plans, and you build onto them with your own chosen materials. For instance, I am currently using the Usborne Ancient History encyclopedia as my spine for history, geography, and social studies. The spine gives me an order in which to study various subjects. You can make your own or find one. Either way, having a spine to base your studies on can be very helpful for further planning.

When I need information about a particular subject, I look for an encyclopedia or a textbook on the subject. I really want one book that will give me the largest amount of information in one single source. I don't really care how engaging it is, since I mostly need it for ideas and not for teaching text. Nice pictures are a bonus, but not a must. I usually get these from the library in the beginning, until I find the one I want to own. I purchase my favorites to make up my own reference library. Some of my spines are university textbooks bought at used book sales for a few bucks each.

There are several publishers who create quality, single-volume encyclopedias for children on a variety of subjects. Usborne is my favorite. DK comes in a close second. Kingfisher, Scholastic, and National Geographic also put out great encyclopedias for kids. If you don't want to use a children's encyclopedia, you can find used university textbooks at book sales or even your local thrift store for great prices. I often use university textbooks to help me find a list of major topics I want to teach for a certain subject (e.g. earth science or physics). Instead of going with a child's curriculum, I borrow the concepts from those higher-level textbooks and then take out the high-level mathematics that make them difficult for kids at younger ages.

If you can't find a book that will work for you, you can always do an Internet search for a list of appropriate topics. Many professors and teachers will share their plans online for a variety of subjects. For things like art and music, I often gather a list of artists or musicians I want to study (between eighteen and thirty-six, depending on how often I plan to cover it or how long I want to study each artist). Once I have that list together, I can start making more definite plans about projects or things to listen to.

Have you chosen a spine or a main book that will help you teach your subject? If you don't plan to use a spine, do you have a list of topics you will be covering?

DIY Curriculum Step #3: Split it up.

The spine or list you chose is going to give you a broad overview of your year. For this step, you'll want to break it up into manageable parts. There are two ways to do this. If you're using a children's encyclopedia as your spine, the easiest way is to count the number of pages you want to get through during your year and then divide by 36 (the number of weeks) to find out how many pages to cover each week. Make this a math assignment for one of your kids if you don't want to do the math yourself. Bonus points if you do it by hand and round to the nearest whole number.

If you have a list of topics to cover, then you'll want to organize them into some sort of order. How many weeks will you work on each topic? Is there a certain order to all those topics that makes sense to you? This part will require a little finesse as you prioritize your chosen topics. You might want to give two or three weeks to a certain topic, but cover two or three other topics together in a single week.

In some cases, you might be combining both ideas. You might use a spine for a certain portion of your year, and then lists of chosen topics for the rest.

In the next two sections, I'll show you how I put together my history and science plans this year. My history plans were all built on an encyclopedia for a spine. My biology plans started with just a list of topics until I found spines for some parts and made up my own for the rest. I hope that by showing you my process, it might help you see how to manage it for yourself on whatever subject or topic you want to teach.

Have you divided up your spines by the number of pages you need to cover each week? Have you given an order to your main topics that makes sense to you?

DIY Curriculum Step #4: Find your key topics.

This step requires a lot of paper and ink, or a computer if you can't read your own handwriting (you know who you are). Depending on how in-depth you will go or how much you plan to branch off into other subjects, I recommend having a sheet of paper for every week you're planning. I can sometimes get away with dividing a sheet into two or three sections and using a section for each week of plans. However, I find that my space-saving endeavors often fail and I'm left with a maze of scribbles and minuscule notes that leave me puzzled for days after.

If you are using topic lists from other textbooks or for things like artist studies, then you've already done most of this step. You know the major things you'll be covering. If you haven't already put those into an ordered thirty-six-week list, you can do it now.

If you chose to split your year up by pages, you'll want to find and write down the main areas of study that will be covered in each of those sections in your spine. This could be as easy as writing down subject headers. When I split out a grammar book, for instance, I might focus on a single part of speech each week. For history, I take quite a few notes during this step. Rather than pick only one topic, I search through the text for several key words—people, places, and things—to focus on.

You'll see more specifically how I do this in my history example, but the gist of it is this: Start at the beginning of your chosen encyclopedia or book and count out the number of pages you need to cover for the first week. You figured out how many pages to cover in step three above. Now you're actually going to look at those pages.

For each group of pages, write down the key words, people, topics, or concepts that will be covered during that section. These notes will give you a launching point to find supplementary material and projects that will make those pages come alive for your kids. Do this for your entire spine. Yes, it's a lot. No, it won't take you as long as you think it will. Just skim the text for keywords and write those down.

As you go through each section, adjust the number of pages you'll cover for that week. If your calculations told you that you have to cover five pages a week to get through your text, you can consider it an average. You might notice that it makes more sense to do a short section of only three or four pages one week, whereas another section of eight pages looks easy. You might decide that one section is so interesting that you want to spend several weeks on it. As you make notes about themes and topics, start adjusting these page sections to make them fit better with your plans.

You might get to the end of your topic notes and realize you only have thirty weeks of plans. Or maybe you get to the end, and you have forty-two weeks' worth of things to cover. If you have more than thirty-six weeks of plans, you'll need to make some adjustments. You might need to combine things or cut things out. If it seems like way too much, you might opt to cut your curriculum in half and cover half of it this year and half the next. You have a lot of options for how you want to manage it.

If you have fewer than thirty-six weeks of plans, but the number is not significantly smaller, you might decide to leave it as is so you have some wiggle room. Many times, I'll plan only thirty or thirty-two weeks of a curriculum for the year. That gives me several extra weeks for review, allows me to finish early, or gives me the chance to take a week off from a certain subject without feeling like I've gotten behind.

Do you have a comprehensive list of main topics you'll be studying for your subject this year? Will it cover thirty-six weeks or fewer? Do you have a broad overview of what you will cover each week?

DIY Curriculum Step #5: Brainstorm supplementary ideas.

This next step can be as streamlined or as complicated as you want it to be. If you're a creative idea person, you'll probably love this step. If you just want it to be done and over with, you don't have to take too long. I try not to spend too much time here. This should be an "off the top of your head" type of list. The true goal is to have a useful list of ideas to make your search for books and resources a little easier.

Look at your list of topic ideas or keywords from your spine, and take a second to think about each one. Jot down a few notes about things you could do to learn about that topic. For instance, let's say one of your key topics is Ancient Egypt. For the sake of simplicity, let's say you're doing the entire Ancient Egyptian timeline in one chunk. You might make a list like this:

-Make a pyramid out of paper or sugar cubes

-Mummify something (Hot dog? Chicken?)

-Visit a museum with a mummy exhibit

-Learn about modern day Egypt

-Find the Nile on a map

-Study floods and how they change landscapes

-Learn emergency preparedness for floods

-Make bricks

-Draw or color pictures of pharaohs

-Learn about desert biomes

-Learn about hieroglyphs

-Learn about Egyptian gods and goddesses and their mythology

I imagine that you had other ideas as you read through those, too. Once you start the brainstorming process, you'll often get more ideas as you go. That's half the fun. The real trick is not to think too hard about it. Just write down the first ideas you have, without deciding if they're good or bad. Don't feel like you have to have a certain number of ideas to pass. Just write down whatever comes to mind and then move on to the next thing.

For some topics (Mesopotamia, anyone?), you may not be able to think of anything offhand. That's okay. Just move on to the next thing.

Do you have your list of keyword topics ready for your chosen subject? Let's go hunting for resources.

DIY Curriculum Step #6: Find resources for your studies.

Thanks to the age of the Internet, I can plan a fantastic school year while sitting in my pajamas, listening to Korean pop music, and eating M&Ms. Homeschoolers are spoiled right now, do you realize that? We've come a long way from the days my mother-in-law tells me about, when their idea of a curriculum sale was dumpster diving at the public school when teachers cleared out their old books. We have hundreds, if not thousands, of different curriculum options to choose from. We have online forums and blogs and catalogs where we can read reviews, look inside books, and chat with other homeschoolers from countries around the world.

I can browse the library catalog for every library in my area without leaving the house or getting paper cuts from the card catalog. I can buy supplies and have them on my doorstep two days later. I can watch videos, read books, print project ideas, and organize my entire year in a spreadsheet without paying for anything beyond my Internet bill and the cost of ink cartridges, which are also delivered whenever I need them. Now, if I could only figure out how to get the Internet to fold my laundry for me, I'd be set.

Finding the resources you want to use for your studies is the fun part, in my opinion. Even though it's the most time-consuming part of the planning process, it's also the most exciting. This is the part of the planning process when I forget to make dinner and start mumbling odd phrases that make no sense to anyone, including myself. I tend to make my family a little crazy when I get here. You might want to make sure you have some quick meals stored in the freezer if you tend to get stuck in research mode. Last year, I set time limits and only allowed myself certain times of the day to work on this. In the past, I might have devoted an entire week of late nights to searching and scouring and scheming, without showering or sleeping. I don't recommend it.

Pace yourself for this part, but have fun.

How you go about your research is totally up to you. Because I have more time than money, I look for free resources first. My favorite source for free is my local library.

If your first thought upon reading the word library is a musty, dark building guarded by a silver-haired lady who glares at you upon arrival, you might need to rethink your view of libraries. Modern libraries are full of many wonderful things, and the books are just the tip of the iceberg. My library's website gives me music downloads, audiobooks, access to language learning apps and programs, databases full of educational resources for any subject I can think of, scientific research, magazines, and DVDs. All of these things are totally free for me to use at any time, as long as they're available. Inside the library, I get free computer use, free Wi-Fi, free printing and copying access, and free use of their conference rooms to teach art or writing lessons (after signing up and agreeing to their terms of use, of course). Apart from all the technology, there are several other priceless resources available to me. They are the librarians who are knowledgeable about the resources available and who are always willing to help with research, ideas, and book recommendations. If I don't know how to find something, one of them almost always has an idea of how to help.

Because I love my library so much, it's the first place I look for materials for my homeschool year. I use the website (also called the Online Catalog) to search for books, videos, and other resources related to my teaching topics. Depending on your library's catalog, you might be able to run advanced searches for only children's or juvenile resources if you get too many book results for a certain topic.

If I find a book or video that looks like it will work for us, I take a trip to my favorite source for reviews: Amazon.com. I look up the book there, read a few reviews to see if it will be a good fit, and use the Look Inside function to browse through the table of contents and a few pages. I don't do this for every possible book or resource, but I do it for many of them.

Sometimes, a search for one book on Amazon will bring up another book with better reviews on the same or similar topics. If that happens, I'll go back and see if the library has the better book. If so, I add that to my list instead.

As I research, I write down the titles of books and DVDs that my library has that will be relevant to our studies. I also put things on my Amazon wish list if I find something I absolutely want but that the library doesn't have. Many times, I will send the library a request to purchase these materials. Did you know that librarians actually kind of like it when you do this? I had no idea. They're always looking for suggestions for new books to purchase. It's a pleasant surprise when you request a purchase and the library buys it for you and adds it to your account so you get the first check out.

After I have two or three books or videos listed for any given topic, I move on to the next thing on my list and keep searching.

What about things like art or science that are harder to teach from books alone? If I'm working through a list of artists I'd like to study and I want projects to help me teach about them, I hit Google with a search for "{artist name} art project for kids" or visit one of my favorite blogs for art projects. If you are a Pinterest addict, this is right up your alley. Start browsing all those homeschool and educator boards for ideas for all those hands-on projects you want to do.

As you find projects, books, videos, and other resources for your learning, write them down in your notebook or on a computer document. You should have a running list going of all the topics you're working on. I almost always find resources for things that I know we'll be studying in later weeks when I'm working through the first topics of my list. Quite often, I'll find an author or series that has books on a number of topics we might be studying. In that case, a single search can provide me with a list of resources for several different weeks at a time.

Because of the likelihood of finding projects or books that fit any number of your chosen subjects for the year, I highly recommend doing this process in a short amount of time—no more than a couple of days if you can manage it. Once you've started the process and you have all the ideas taking up precious space in your mind, keep going until it's done. If you spread this out over a long period, you'll be more likely to forget and then have to spend extra time searching again for things you've already found.

Have you chosen projects, books, DVDs, worksheets, or other necessary resources? These are the things that will make up your curriculum for the year. Fill in any large gaps now. If you find that you went a little overboard, feel free to cross out a few things here or there. Make sure that the lists of things you've chosen are worth spending your time, energy, or money on. Once you're ready, let's move on and put these ideas in a format you can use.

DIY Curriculum Step #7: Manage your resource lists.

This step could be part of Step 6 if you manage it correctly. Sometimes I do, and sometimes I don't. During my first year of planning with this method, I used colored index cards. For each subject I was planning, I used a different color of index card so I could easily find all my science or history plans at a glance.

In the upper right-hand corner, I wrote the week number and then circled it. I had blue cards for history numbered 1through 36, green cards for science numbered 1through 36, and pink cards for art numbered 1 through 36. Across the top line, I wrote the main topic or course of study for that week for that subject. For history, this included the page numbers of the encyclopedia I was using for my spine, plus two or three keywords.

On the lower lines of the index cards, I wrote the titles and authors of the books I planned to check out from the library. For science, I listed books to borrow from the library. I also wrote the title of the book and page number for any experiments we planned to do. If there was a website I wanted to visit, I wrote the web address. I also wrote a list of all the supplies needed to perform any planned experiments. My art cards were similar, with notes about the art project we would be doing and lists of needed supplies for it.

The great thing about using index cards in this way is that they are easily sortable. You can get a week behind in history and a week ahead in science, and you can still see everything you need at any given time. As I was preparing for those weeks, I would often shuffle through my cards, purchasing supplies and requesting library resources about two weeks in advance so we would have them when they were needed.

Why don't I continue to use index cards? My first excuse is that I want to see everything I'm doing for any given week all at once on one page. The truth is, I'm too lazy to be quite that color-coded and organized anymore.

Two years ago, I put together a thirty-six-page color-coded document in Google Drive (I think it was Google Docs then) that had all of my plans for each subject along with book and supply lists for each subject. It contained all the links to my art projects (along with thumbnail pictures of the finished projects!) and science experiments right there in the document. It was lovely. It was a work of art, to be honest. I still open it up just to admire it and laugh at myself sometimes.

I don't get quite that pretty about it anymore, for a number of reasons. Putting everything in a final computerized document makes it difficult for me to move things around, and sometimes I really need to shift a subject or alter my plans without adjusting an entire thirty-six-page document. I also realized that I am a paper person. I don't mind having things backed up on the computer, but I like having paper to look at and scribble notes on.

My current system is to make separate documents in my Google Drive folder for each subject that I'm planning. I still put the week number, encyclopedia page numbers, and topic headers across one line; then I list the books and needed resources underneath.

After I've put together all of my subjects for the year, I print out these sheets and cut them into weekly segments. In my weekly plans notebook (which you'll be making in the section on Calendars), I tape in these weekly blocks. It's hideous. I wouldn't show it off unless someone asked to see that ugly notebook in particular. But it works wonderfully. As my plans start to come together, I can easily shift the plans for each subject around. I can adjust things if I see that a week is too heavy with events or if I've planned a huge amount of work for every single subject.

Why do I tell you all this? I want you to see that even using the same planning process, there is no right or wrong way to get these plans into a form you can use. You can use index cards if that works for you. You can have a document on your computer if that works better. You can make things beautiful with hand-drawn stationery and little illustrations. Whatever works for you to get it done is great. What you really should care about is having these plans in a place where (1) they will not get lost, (2) you can reference them when you need to buy or borrow resources and (3) you have a backup if needed.

Are all your plans put together in a way that lets you see at a glance what you need to buy or borrow? At this point, you should feel ready for the school year ahead, at least in the subject you just finished planning. Now it's just a matter of getting it mixed in with everything else on your calendar and then diving in to your school year.

DIY Curriculum Step #8: Purchase or borrow supplies.

This is the last step to getting your curriculum together for the year. If you are planning to borrow your supplies from the library or another source, make sure you request them far enough in advance that you're not left in a lurch when the time comes. I request my library books about two weeks before I plan to use them, because my books often come from other libraries in the system and might take a week or more to arrive. When I'm in the middle of schooling, I visit the library once a week and manage my requests and holds on the same day so I can stay on top of them.

Purchase any of the spines you'll be using. If you're planning your own curricula for several subjects at the same time, you can add anything you need to your shopping list and keep an eye out for them at local or online sales.

You might also opt to purchase all your supplies for subjects like science and art now. This can be a great idea if you have a coupon for a percentage off an entire purchase or can get free shipping with a minimum purchase. You'll just need to double-check that you still have those supplies when it comes time to do your project. If your kids are like mine, those precious supplies might become art or science long before they're scheduled to.

Do you feel a bit more confident about planning your own curricula now? In the next few sections, I'll show you more specifically how this process looks for me as I plan history and science every year. If you're the type to need more details about it before jumping out on your own, I hope these examples will help you better understand the process.

Do-It-Yourself History

In this section, I'll show you a step-by-step example of how I build my plans for a year of history, and how I use the topics to branch into other subjects for school.

DIY Steps

1. Choose what to teach and how to teach it.
2. Find your spine.
3. Split it up.
4. Find your key topics.
5. Brainstorm supplementary ideas.
6. Find resources for your studies.
7. Manage your resource lists.
8. Purchase or borrow supplies

Example Step #1: Choose what to teach and how to teach it.

For the last several years, I have based the majority of my school plans around the four-year history cycle outlined in the book The Well-Trained Mind by Susan Wise Bauer. The four-year cycle has a simple premise: teach history chronologically from the beginning up to the present over four years. In the first year, children would study Ancient History through the fall of Rome, approximately 5000 BC to AD 400. In year two, they study the Medieval period to the early Renaissance, 400 to 1600. In year three, they study the Renaissance to the early Modern era, 1600 to 1850. The fourth year takes them from 1850 to the present day. At the end of four years, after going through the Ancients, the Renaissance, the early Modern age, and the present era, they go back and do it all over again. Each cycle adds more to the picture until the students are studying the original texts and documents written during those eras. By the time your children complete twelve years of schooling, they've been through all of World History three times and probably have a good grasp on the cause-and-effect issues surrounding world events.

I wasn't entirely convinced when I first started. I didn't even like history when I was growing up. It was boring compared to more exciting subjects like math and science. However, once I started teaching my kids through chronological world history, it came to life in a way it never had before. Even though my daughter is two years younger than my son, I keep her in the same year of history to make it easier on everyone. It makes for some wonderful discussions and the kids make connections that I had never seen before.

Two years ago, while studying the Industrial Revolution, my son came up with an idea for a form of government that did away with all the abuses of the industrial era. It would share the wealth of resources with the people who did all the work and take control out of the hands of the wealthy land and factory owners. Does that sound familiar? The very next lesson in history was about Karl Marx and the rise of Communism.

We also had some eye-opening moments about Columbus and his westward travels in search for the Indies. I had never known it before, or maybe I hadn't connected it, but at the time, the Silk Road that connected China (and India) to Europe had been taken hostage by the Ottomans, who were angry about the Crusades and distrustful of doing trade with the West. Sailors from England, Spain, and Portugal took to their ships to try and find another trade route, especially one that cut some time off the standard trip around Africa.

After a few years of this, I've discovered that history is really exciting, and quite predictable. We see patterns all over the place. It's not a series of names and dates to memorize, but a long story full of colorful characters and strange adventures.

Another thing I noticed, as my kids got older and added more subjects to their studies, is how well I could combine other subjects with our history studies. Geography and social studies are easy to plan around the historical locations and cultures we study in history. Handwriting copywork comes out of famous speeches, literature, and documents from the historical period we're working through. Occupational education happens when we talk about and act out the various vocations and economic systems of past societies. My kids like to imagine they are peasants. They constantly stage uprisings and riots in an attempt to usurp my tyrannical powers over them. I'm a very powerful monarch, unfortunately for them. As we get into the Renaissance and Modern eras, music and art are full of fantastic patterns as artists build on the work of others and musical styles mirror the cultures around them. Starting from the beginning and tracking the evolution of human expression week-by-week over a four-year period can be a wonderful experience.

What do you do if you're teaching kids that are different ages? If you have more than one child of school age and you're starting this process after the first grade, I can tell you that it's very easy to combine multiple kids in a study of the same period of history. In fact, the best part about this entire process is how flexible it is for your family and interests. If you have one child who loves bugs, dirt, and war (my son), and another child who loves fashion and cooking and animals (my daughter), you can easily choose materials for your studies that will interest each of them.

I started the cycle when my son was in the first grade. Instead of starting over with my daughter when she started first, I just started her where we were in the third year. She'll still study the full cycle three times if we continue it through her high school years. Plus, she had the advantage of doing many of those early projects with us even before I had her "doing school."

If you want more information about the four-year history cycle and reasoning behind it, check out The Well-Trained Mind by Susan Wise Bauer. It's one of my favorite guides to home education, even though I pick and choose which parts of it I do in my own home.

Because I've used this system so successfully, I'm going to base my plans around my second run-through of the cycle. We're back in the Ancients again for the second time.

Example Step #2: Find your spine.

It took me a little while to narrow down my options for spines for world history. Many homeschoolers swear by the Kingfisher encyclopedias. I found that the Usborne and DK encyclopedias worked a little better with my style. The text in the Usborne encyclopedias reads better as a story, but the DK encyclopedia tends to have better pictures and more information connecting different events to each other.

Over the four years, I have used the Usborne encyclopedias *Ancient World, Medieval,* and *The Last 500 Years* as well as the DK *History of the World*). For this example, I'll be using pages from the Usborne *Ancient World* Encyclopedia.

Example Step #3: Split it up.

First of all, I made a major leap in the very first part. If I were coming to this process knowing only that I needed to teach "History," then I'd have some decisions to make. Do I want to teach World History or American History? Do I want to devote my history studies to the history of my family or community or city or state? Those are all decisions you might need to make. For me, I teach everything as part of World History. I also have built-in divisions since I adopted the four-year cycle. So, it's already split into certain sections of history for me.

Since I know I'm going to teach the Ancients through the Fall of Rome, I have a history encyclopedia that covers that period in particular. If I were using a full encyclopedia of all of world history, like my DK *History of the World*, I would need to find the beginning and end of the particular section that covers the first civilizations and goes through about AD 500.

In the Usborne *Ancient World* book, the actual content I planned to teach from starts on page 3 and ends on page 91. That's eighty-eight pages of teachable information. If I do the math (I cheated and used a calculator) and divide 88 pages by 36 weeks of school, I get 2.4. For the sake of my safety and sanity, I rounded that to whole numbers and decided that I needed to get through two or three pages of information each week to make it to the end. That's not too bad.

Step #4: Find your key topics.

With my awesome notebook in hand, I started skimming through the sections in my encyclopedia. I started on page three and flipped through two or three pages. I decided three pages looked pretty easy. Those three pages included three separate sections: "When? Where? How?," "The First Farmers," and "The First Towns." Since it's the very beginning of known history, I decided it made sense to do it all during the same week. On my notebook page, I jotted down "Week 1. pp 3-5: first farmers and towns." Then I made a short list of subjects from the pages:

> *BC/AD or BCE/CE*
> *Archaeology*
> *Fertile Crescent*
> *Domestic animals*
> *Jericho*
> *Death & Burial*
> *Catal Huyuk*

That was more than enough to get me started, so I moved on to the next week.

> *Week 2. Pages 6-8: First Civilizations & Crafts & Trade*
> *Sumer*
> *Mud-brick making*
> *Ziggurats*
> *City-states*
> *Invention of writing*
> *Merchants and trading*
> *Invention of the wheel*

See how that works? I just wrote down the main ideas, keywords, or topics from the text in a way I could use to find more information about each of those things. This process took me about half an hour for this particular encyclopedia when I was getting my plans together this year. Depending on what you use for your spine, it probably won't take very long to skim the text and find your main ideas. Larger textbooks might be more difficult. For very involved textbooks, I often take sub headers as keywords to save some time.

What do you do if you come to a section that doesn't easily break into the number of pages you've chosen? For instance, pages 12-13 in my book deal with Mummies and Pyramids, and then 14-15 move into the Cities of the Indus Valley. The pages following that shift all the way over to Europe's First Villages. None of these fit together very easily. In this case, I chose to cover only two pages a week. In fact, I chose to spend two weeks on Mummies and Pyramids, and then combined subjects further in the book to make up for it.

Example Step #5: Brainstorm supplementary ideas.

I didn't do a lot of brainstorming this year. I had a pretty clear idea about what I wanted to see in my weeks, and still had a lot of resources from our last time through the history cycle. However, I'll give you an example of how I might take those key topics and run with them across several different subjects.

The very first idea I wrote down was about the abbreviations BC, AD, BCE, CE. What could I do with that topic? If I were brainstorming ideas, my list in my notebook would look like this:

~ build a timeline

~ create a number line and show the kids how BC works like negative numbers (math)

~ teach the meaning behind those abbreviations and explain why some people prefer one pair of them over the other (Latin, social studies)

~ talk about the different types of calendar systems, like the Gregorian, Julian, and lunar calendars (history, social studies, science, math)

Next on the list? Archaeology. Let's do a quick brainstorm for this one.

~ check out a book on archaeology (reading, history, science)

~ go on a "dig" through our house to see what we can learn about our family (social science)

~ visit a museum or an actual archaeology dig (history, science, social science)

Good. Now on to the Fertile Crescent. This one is, pardon the pun, rich with resource ideas.

~ find the Fertile Crescent on a map (geography)

~ notice that it's right in the middle of Iraq and Syria (geography)

~ talk about current events in those countries (social science, history, cultures)

~ talk about the importance of fresh water in the sustaining of life (science)

~ talk about how most civilizations rise up around bodies of fresh drinking water (history, social science)

~ discuss farming and gardening (science, social science)

~ plant two plants and water one with fresh water and one with salt water (science)

~ read the story of the Garden of Eden, which was believed to be between the Tigris and Euphrates rivers, in your chosen Biblical translation (Biblical studies, literature)

~ visit a local river and observe the life that lives around it (science)

~ draw, paint, or glue together a picture that includes a river and the type of plants that might grow around it (art)

How about Domestic Animals?

~ talk about the difference between wild and domestic animals

~ visit a farm and learn how much work goes into caring for the animals and crops

~ have each of the kids choose an animal to study and have them write a report about it

~ talk about wild animals that would be interesting or strange as domestic pets

Death and Burial is on my list, too. That sounds creepy. When I looked at these sections during our first year, I shied away from these topics. I didn't want to talk about them. However, as we read the encyclopedia text, that section caught their eye. The book included a sketch of a burial site for a queen who had been buried along with her servants, several animals, and a hoard of treasure. The kids asked me so many questions about that one tiny section that I really wish I had prepared for it. Since so many of the famous archaeological digs are from large burial sites, these can tell us a lot about a culture and what was important to them. My kids liked knowing how someone might be treated after death, what people believed about what happens after death, and what happens to the people who are left behind when someone dies. This could make for some very interesting social or religious studies if you wanted to get into it.

I think you get the idea. Any single one of the topics listed could create an entire unit for our week, complete with several different subjects to study. There are ideas for math, writing, science, art, social studies, and geography. That's not too bad for a few pages from a children's history encyclopedia.

Example Step #6: Find resources for your studies.

After I had my ideas together, I went searching for resources. I started at the library website. Among other things, I discovered that there are absolutely no children's books about Catal Huyuk (and even if there were, would I really want to spend our precious time reading it? I'm not sure). I searched on Google instead and found many clear images of the location and a few kids' websites with more information. As I kept searching for things, I found a book at the library called *Archaeologists Dig for Clues* and immediately added it to my list. As I gathered the resources I already owned, I found a timeline I had purchased a few years ago and promptly forgotten about. I made a note to put it on the wall during the first week. At this point, I decided I was done with the first week of plans. We had a book, an activity, and some decent websites to add to our reading from the encyclopedia.

Does that seem to you like it's not very much? Here are a few other things I know about my first week of school: we're almost always a little off kilter, and getting down to the nitty-gritty of math and reading and writing is going to take more time than I want it to. I know that I'll be pretty lucky if I get through the history reading without a few eye rolls and bored sighs. I also know that putting up the timeline has the potential to be a time-consuming project, but if I can catch the kids' interest with it, it also has the potential to be a fantastic learning tool during that week and the rest of year.

Because I knew that would be enough for week one, I moved on to week two and kept going.

This part took me about two days, spending a few hours on it each day. I spent more time looking for good resources for some of my larger units, like the ones on Ancient China, Ancient Japan, and the Greeks and Romans. I knew that those cultures and their histories would be important to understand as we moved forward in our history studies, so my lists of books, projects, and ideas were much longer for those sections.

Example Step #7: Manage your resource lists.

The previous step left me with a notebook full of crossed-out book titles, starred notes about activity ideas, website names, streaming media to check out on Netflix or Amazon Prime or PBS, and a variety of doodles and swear words mixed in with whatever else I found at the time. I might be kidding about the swear words.

From here, I created a new document in my Homeschool Plans folder in Google Drive. I think I called it something really creative like "2014-2015 History plans." Here's a copy of the first three weeks of my plans so you can see how they look:

Spine: Usborne Ancient History

Key: * = activity book ^ = audio book () = DVD ? = buy

1. 3-5: when where how - first farmers - first towns

Children Just Like Me (Kindersley)

Archaeologists Dig for Clues (Kate Duke)

The Tigris and Euphrates (Gary Miller)

2. 6-9: First civilizations - crafts & trade - kings & war

Ox, House, Stick (Don Robb)

Gilgamesh the King (Ludmila Zeman)

Science in Ancient Mesopotamia (Carol Moss)

3 & 4. 10-13: farmers of the Nile - mummies & pyramids

We're Sailing Down the Nile (Laurie Krebs)

The Great Pyramid (Elizabeth Mann)

*Ancient Egyptians and Their Neighbors (Marian Broida)

^Egyptian Treasures: Mummies & Myths (Jim Weiss)

My favorite part about this is that it feels complete at this point. The handwritten notes always need a little deciphering, but this document will serve as my brain when it comes time to make this learning thing happen. It's clean. I can print a few copies and cut them up or scribble notes on them, but I also have the backup on my computer (and any other device with access to Drive).

Example Step #8: Purchase or borrow supplies.

History tends to be an easy subject on the budget, but there are always a few books I really want to use that aren't available from the library. I either put in a request for the library to purchase them, ask for an inter-library loan (which might come with a small fee), or I purchase them for myself. These usually end up on one of my wish lists until I'm ready to order all my supplies for the year.

If you plan to do a lot of activities as part of your history studies, you might need to purchase supplies for your projects. I find that I'm always gathering things like clay, felt, costume fabric, specialty food items, construction paper, and cardboard boxes for history projects. Those things can be acquired or purchased in the week or two leading up to your project as well.

Now I have a full year of history planned out. It takes me a few days from start to finish, but it feels great once it's done. History is fairly easy since I start from an encyclopedia that I plan to read with the kids. I can choose to do the bare minimum and just read the text, or I can add in all the extras on any given week, and they'll still learn something.

How do you manage when you don't have a spine that you'll be reading? In the next section, I'll show you how I build my science plans using a mix of topical ideas and spines.

Do-It-Yourself Science

When I planned science this year, I used the same set of steps as I did for history. I chose what to teach, created my own spine with a topic list, brainstormed ideas, looked for resources, put together a list of things to buy or borrow, and then put it all together in my weekly notebook so I could manage everything. The main difference is how I chose what I wanted to teach and how I managed without having a spine to teach from. I chose topics to study and built my yearly curriculum around a series of units instead of an encyclopedia. If seeing the planning process in action is helpful to you, then read on.

Example Step #1: Choose what to teach and how to teach it.

Science is another one of those broad categories that could be taught in dozens of different ways on hundreds of different topics. In my four years of planning my own science curriculum, I have come to know what I want: I want a lot of hands-on experiments and/or great photographs to study, I don't want it dumbed down too much, and I want to teach it in an order that makes sense and keeps ideas connected to each other.

In my experience, people have a lot of different ideas about what constitutes science, and that can often be a barrier to teaching it. When I tell people we're learning chemistry or physics, I often get the same kind of look I get from people when I mention we're doing beginning algebra. Algebra is just a way of balancing equations and showing that one side is exactly the same as the other. Working with that knowledge helps you discover how to find things that are missing from one side of the other. Chemistry is just a way of understanding the main building blocks of things, and discovering how those building blocks work together and how they break apart. At the very basis of each are concepts even young elementary students can understand.

In my mind, there are four different sciences: biology, chemistry, physics, and earth science. You might have a different division than I do. I know some people say only the first three are different from one another and earth science is a combination of all of them. I do think that all of the sciences are intertwined together, but I think they all encompass different things. If you distill them down to their most basic ideas, they are a little easier to understand. Biology is the study of things that are alive. Chemistry is the study of elements and how they mix together to compose everything we know. Physics is the study of how things move. Earth science is the study of the earth: what it's made of, how it exists in its current form, and how it moves as it does through space.

If you think of each of the sciences on those levels, they are easier to teach. Physics does not have to consist of complicated equations. A child does not have to know the gravitational constant in order to experience the way gravity works. A child does not have to know the molecular composition of various salts in order to witness how they dissolve and then recrystallize in different forms.

Depending on your goals for science, you might decide you want to teach any number of things. I hope that looking through my plans might help you figure out how you want to do it for yourself. You might even teach science through a unit that's based entirely on some other subject. Many of my friends who do unit studies don't do science as its own curriculum, but attach it to their other studies. That totally works, too.

I teach science in a four-year cycle, just like history. I teach biology, then chemistry, then physics, then earth science. That helps me decide the big subject for my year, but I still have to break it down.

This year, I was back in the first-year cycle with biology again. At first, I considered recycling my topics and lists from my first time through it. The first time through, our entire year of biology was built on the classifications of plants and animals, starting from single-celled organisms and increasing in complexity until we were studying humans. This year, I didn't want to do it exactly the same way, so I had to spend some extra energy figuring it out. I knew I wanted to do a unit on microbiology because of my son's interest in cells and their structures. I also knew I wanted to spend a long period of time studying animals, followed by several weeks studying the human body. At this point in my planning, I didn't know much more than that.

Example Step #2: Find your spine.

I came to this step with just a few ideas for what I wanted. I knew from experience that I wanted to include a lot of hands-on work, a lot of great photographs, and some fun picture books that explained complex topics in ways that we all could understand. That's all I knew at the time, so I started looking for my spine, either in the form of a book or in the form of a list of subjects to cover.

As I looked into the different ways to go about teaching microbiology, zoology, and human anatomy and physiology, I happened upon a few that I liked.

At first, the thought of teaching microbiology made my eyes glaze over a bit. My son had been asking to study microbiology ever since my brother gave him a college textbook as a gift. You would be surprised how often my son receives science textbooks as gifts. You would be even more surprised to discover how much the boy adores these things. Still, microbiology seemed daunting to teach at elementary levels.

I decided to flip through my brother's old textbook, just to get some ideas about what to cover. I was fully prepared to be overwhelmed by a lot of science I didn't understand. Instead, I found several topics that looked like they could be interesting for the kids. Animal cells and all their organelles could be really fun. I remembered seeing Pinterest projects to create cell models using foods. I remembered how much I loved seeing inside a plant cell for the first time and watching all that chlorophyll go traveling by, like traffic on a freeway. I decided that the main topics of interest for my kids would probably be plant and animal cells, DNA, and genetics.

What part of this ended up being my spine? It might appear that the microbiology textbook was my spine, but in all honesty, I put it away a few days later (mostly because the boy started dreaming up nefarious experiments involving clones, spliced DNA, and stem cells).

In a way, I used that microbiology textbook to help me create my own version of a spine. The list of four topics to study was my actual spine here.

Once I had my microbiology idea settled, I moved on to deciding how to manage our study of animals. The last time we studied animals, I went through them based on taxonomy. We started with microbes, progressed to fish, then insects, then reptiles, then birds, and so on. I didn't feel like I wanted to do it that way this time, as I felt the kids had a decent grasp on classification.

I was a little lost at this point, so I decided to consult the children. Consulting the children can be a very dangerous thing to do if you're trying to make big life decisions, because they don't beat around the bush. On rare occasions, I have regretted even asking them, but the vast majority of the time, I find that they have great, creative ideas about things.

"What animals do you want to learn about this year?" I asked. My daughter started listing a number of animals: polar bears, penguins, seals, whales, and walruses. My son started spouting off animals like ocelots, wolves, cows, sheep, and pigs—all creatures that are part of Minecraft, a video game we all enjoy playing.

My son's mention of Minecraft got me thinking about how to wrap our biology study around the game, since that could be fun. However, there are only a limited number of plants and creatures in the game. If you've never played Minecraft, it's a game that is built on a series of simple blocks that you can move around and alter. We like to refer to it as interactive LEGO. Each individual Minecraft world contains a number of different biomes or ecosystems, and depending on what biome you are in, you can find particular plants and elements that you can't find anywhere else in the game. There are desert, jungle, plains, taiga (snowy), and forest biomes.

As I thought more about it, I realized my daughter had mentioned only polar animals. Then I had an idea that had very little to do with Minecraft and a lot to do with the biomes of the earth.

I started looking into complete ecosystems so that I could teach the plants and animals based on where they live and how they live together. I did several Google searches on biomes and ecosystems, making lists of the various types. My searches led me to discover a book, the *First Nature Encyclopedia* by DK, that covers the major biomes in a logical order. In a flash of sudden insight, I realized that I already owned this book. You might be very surprised to discover that this is not the first time this has happened. There have been a few instances when I've really needed a particular book for some study and then found the book sitting on my own bookshelves. In other news, I also get lost in my own apartment sometimes.

I decided to use the *First Nature Encyclopedia* for my spine, and listed out the biomes we would study: polar, cool forests, rainforests, grasslands, deserts, mountains & caves, freshwater habitats, and ocean habitats.

Then I moved on to the human body. Despite owning several quality children's human body encyclopedias (I checked the bookshelves first, this time), there wasn't a single one I wanted to use in its entirety. I wanted to teach the human body based on the various systems. I searched online and found a decent list. I wrote down the systems we would study: skeletal, muscular, nervous, respiratory, circulatory, digestive, urinary, immune, lymphatic, endocrine, and reproductive.

In case you're curious, the only science I've never messed with is chemistry. I rather adore the book *Fizz, Bubble, Flash* from the Williamson Kids Can! series. That book teaches the elements of the periodic table through a great mix of engaging text and easy-to-do experiments, and the order makes wonderful sense to me. Other than that, I have made my own lists for biology, physics, and earth science.

Example Steps #3 & 4: Split it up & Find your key topics.

Because I was working from a series of topic lists for science, I didn't have to split any spines to find page numbers we would study during particular weeks. I basically created my spines and split them out at the same time. What I really needed to do was work them into a set of thirty-six-week plans so I could see at a glance what topic we would be covering during a certain week of the school year.

There are times when you might skip both of these steps as well. For instance, if you were planning an artist or musician study, you might make a list of the people you want to learn more about. In that case, your list would serve as your spine, it would already be split into key topics, and you would know whether you were going to do one person a month, one every two weeks, or one a week. It's already laid out in a weekly schedule for you. If you need to tweak the order a bit to get it set out the way you want it, this is the step where you would do that.

The task here is to put your list of topics in an order that makes sense to you so that you have thirty-six weeks' worth of plans set out.

As I worked through my science lists, as I do every year, I asked myself a few questions.

1. How many weeks do I want I spend on each topic?

2. Is there an order to these topics that makes good sense to me?

3. Would some of these topics work better during a certain season of the year, or after or before other topics?

I started by taking my major subjects and putting them in an order that made sense to me. I like the idea of starting at the cellular level, moving on to ecosystems, and then studying the human body in more detail. Perhaps in another year, I might go from cells to human systems to ecosystems, and that would make sense, too. Whatever works best for you.

Since microbiology is only four subjects (plant and animal cells, DNA, and genetics), I decided I would spend a six-week unit on it and add a week for introduction and a week for review and extra projects and games. As I looked at my biomes list, I realized I could spend two weeks on each biome and get sixteen weeks of study. I added two extra weeks for review and projects to give us some wiggle room. With six weeks for microbiology and eighteen weeks for zoology, I had planned for twenty-four weeks of school. The last twelve weeks went to the human body systems.

After deciding on the larger breakdown, I numbered a page of my handy notebook with my week numbers from 1 through 36, and then started listing the topics. The order for microbiology and for the study of biomes was already pretty well set. I just wrote them in, adding the extra review weeks.

Fitting the entire human body into twelve weeks was a little harder. I could easily fit one topic a week and call it good, but the idea of covering the entire nervous system and all five senses in one single week felt daunting. On the other hand, the idea of spending an entire week talking about the lymphatic system seemed excessive, when I could combine it with the immune or endocrine system and get along pretty well. Once I'd chosen what subjects to combine and what subjects to spend more time with, I had a working list that showed me the major science topics we would cover for each of our thirty-six weeks of school.

Example Step #5: Brainstorm supplementary ideas.

This part was streamlined for me this year. Instead of brainstorming for each and every week, I did more of the brainstorming for the overriding ideas. In fact, a great deal of the brainstorming was happening as I was putting together those topic lists. You might have noticed that my chosen topics for microbiology had to do with ideas for experiments or observations I had already seen.

I knew I wanted to create a model of an animal cell, including its organelles. I also knew I had a great video game to play called CellCraft that introduces all those parts and their functions in a fun and interactive way. I thought about borrowing a microscope to examine living plant cells or at least finding a video showing plant cells. I wanted to do a science experiment I've seen to extract DNA from household objects. I wanted to do some worksheets showing the simplification of genetics based on Mendel's pea studies, because my son had been asking for something like that for weeks. In just a few minutes, I'd already filled up my six weeks of plans. I knew I'd want to get a couple of great picture books on each of the subjects, too, so I made a note to search for those. This took less than ten minutes.

I moved on to the eighteen-week study of biomes. At the top level, I knew I wanted to create a large project for each biome we would be studying this year. Because my daughter loves art and crafting so much, I wanted to make this study very fun for her at a hands-on level. I waffled between the idea of crafting dioramas or making posters for each biome before I decided to do a mix of both. After that, I did more brainstorming for each of the biomes. For this part, I jotted down the major plants and animals I knew of from each place, so it would be easier to find books. I didn't want to spend much time at it, but wanted to give myself a short list so I could more easily find resources. For the polar regions, I wrote down polar bears and penguins. For cool forests, I thought of elk, coniferous trees, mushrooms, and badgers. Thanks to the Rio movies, rainforests made me think of macaws, parrots, and tree frogs. I think you get the idea here. Even though this step sounds complex, it takes very little time. It's also incredibly helpful to do it before moving on to looking for resources. I have found that it can be difficult to think of new ideas when you're in the middle of searching for things.

Then it was on to the human body systems, which seemed pretty straightforward. What I really wanted to do was find a hands-on project we could do that demonstrated each of the systems (except for the urinary and reproductive systems—I'm not that crazy). I thought that creating our own skeleton might be fun, and then thought of how we could build the other systems around it. With that idea in mind, and my notes for everything else, I hit the Internet to start finding what I wanted.

Example Step #6: Find resources for your studies.

This step looked exactly the same for science as it did for history. I spent some time with multiple browser tabs open, searching my library's catalog, Amazon reviews, and the various homeschool sites where I could purchase hands-on materials. A search for "hands-on body systems" helped me find the perfect book for my human body studies, in the form of Scholastic's *Body Book*. After looking through reviews and some of the examples in the book, I decided to use it as my spine for my human body studies. It may seem odd that I had to work through all these steps before I could find the book I wanted to use as the basis for my studies, but it's not that rare for me. Sometimes I have to skip a step or two and come back to it when I know more.

I also spent quite a bit of time on Pinterest, looking through projects. I found some great ideas there, including a board game that is built around a life-size demonstration of the circulatory system.

I added the books, videos, and project ideas to each of my topics so I would know what to use when the time came. Some of my topics had only one or two books to use as supplementary materials. The biomes had around a dozen resources each, because I wanted to get separate reading books about many of the more interesting animals and plants. Since I planned to study each biome over a course of two weeks, I reasoned that having a lot of reference books and resources available would be great help in creating projects that show those biomes.

In all, I think this project took about two days from start to finish. Once I had the topics nailed down, searching for resources was the most time-consuming part. However, since I had done so much preliminary work in brainstorming and deciding on how I wanted to go about teaching each topic, I didn't have to waste a lot of time deciding whether a particular book or video would be good or not. I knew what I wanted, and I just had to find those things.

Example Step #7: Manage your resource lists.

Just like with history, I had to decipher my scrawls of ideas so I could type all my science plans into one document. I found that my science plans, like my history plans, had a variety of types of resources like books, videos, hands-on projects, and games. I used the same symbols to help me see which ones were books to get from the library, which were projects to do, and which were DVDs or videos to borrow or stream from various websites.

At this point, I was getting more excited about the year and all the activities we would be doing. When I'm slogging through the hand-written list, it feels daunting, like I will never finish this thing and maybe I should stop trying. Once I get it all typed in, it's as though I've climbed a mountain and have just made it to the top. Now I can see why I was climbing. I can see everything in front of me, now, and it looks like it's going to be fun. Everything is easy from that point. Once the plans are done and typed in, I am ready. Bring on the education!

Example Step #8: Purchase or borrow supplies.

As I looked through my list of science resources, I noticed a few things I needed to purchase right away so I could finalize my plans, but there were also things that could be purchased later in the year. I added supplies and books to my growing list of needed homeschool supplies. Once I finished all my subject planning, I spent a little time shopping online, finding the best prices from my favorite companies until I had several orders put together.

Biology is a lot easier on the budget than the other sciences, at least for my family. The largest expense is usually a membership to a local zoo, or the admission prices to two or three different places over the course of the year. I don't get off this easily every year. For physics, I found that I needed to acquire a lot of extra supplies in order to do experiments involving electricity, magnetism, force, motion, and light. If you're shopping for physics or chemistry, which are usually experiment-intensive, you might be able to find one kit that includes just about everything you need. It's also possible that you can manage it with household supplies you already own, and you only need to make a short list of extras to pick up. I adore hands-on science, so I tend to acquire science supplies wherever I can find them, even I don't have a use for them at the time. If you don't love science like I do, consider getting a kit for your subject that has everything you need. Check the reviews to make sure the kit comes with good instructions and scientific explanations of your experiments.

DIY curriculum review

I hope that the sections on planning your own curriculum are helpful. Since it's such an individualized process, you might need to make some adjustments to my steps. You might need to go about it in a different way or do the steps in a different order. That's okay. What I want you to see is that it is possible to put things together for yourself if you want to. With a little bit of planning and some research, you can put together your own curriculum using mostly free resources. The fun part about creating your own curriculum plans is that you can adjust things as you go and add in all sorts of activities that you know your family will enjoy. The bad part about creating your own curriculum plans is that you have no one to blame if they don't turn out as great as you had hoped.

Another difficult part about creating your own plans, especially those that use borrowed resources, is that keeping up with library holds and staying on track with your plans can take some extra time. After we work on getting things settled in your yearly calendar, I'll show you a few ways to help you keep up and stay with it for the entire year.

Blueprint Sketch #29: If you build it, they will come.

If you couldn't find the right curricula for your needs, it's time to build your own. Make plans for any of the subjects or ideas you don't already have covered. Make sure it's split out to cover about thirty-six weeks of a school year and that you know what resources you will need to buy or borrow in order to make it work. Type it up into a legible final format so you can use it for calendar planning in the next section.

Curricula review

Deciding on curricula is often the hardest step of homeschool planning. If you're at that point right now, don't fret. Finding the right curricula can be a matter of time and experience. For many of the homeschoolers I know, not everything fits right even if they think it will. If you're new to homeschooling, it might take two or three years to really hit your stride. You may need to take a few different choices for a test drive before you find the resources you really like. On the other hand, you may happen upon the perfect thing without searching much, and homeschooling might feel easy to you right from the beginning. That's normal, too.

If you haven't already decided on your curricula or created your own, now is the time. It really helps to have all those things in hand before we start putting it all into your calendar and managing how your time will be spent in the coming months.

~ First, check the list of things you'll be working on this year. Now, check your inventory. What resources do you already have at home or on your computer that you could use for your studies this year?

~ Start a shopping list. You'll refer to this throughout your hunt for curriculum and extra resources. Add things that you haven't purchased yet. You might include things like sign-ups for special programs or registration for classes and events, too.

~ Will you use a boxed curriculum that's already made for you? If so, decide where you want to purchase it from and what levels you want to purchase. Check if you can get a sale price or get on a payment plan if the cost is a hindrance. Double-check that the boxed curriculum will include all the subjects you want to cover. If any are missing, you'll need to plan for those as well. You may be able to find the extras you need from the same retailer and add them individually to your boxed curriculum order.

~ For any subjects you don't already have curricula for, it's time to go hunting. Find your local homeschool groups, conventions, forums, or catalogs to help you find out what curricula are out there that might work with your family and your style. Decide what you'll use and purchase them or add them to your shopping list to purchase at your next opportunity.

~ If you don't find what you're looking for, consider creating your own curriculum. There are quite a few ways to do this. Once you have your plans set, put them in a final format and back them up somewhere. Purchase anything you need, or add resources to your shopping or borrowing lists.

~ Buy your curriculum for the year, add things to wish lists or grocery lists to purchase later, or check to see if your local library has resources you need.

Once you have your entire curriculum in hand for the year, we can finally move on to planning around your calendar.

Part Five: Calendars

Calendar options

You know what values drive your homeschool now, you know what methods you and your children use best, and you've set goals for your year. You know what curriculum you'll be using for each of the subjects you want to teach. Now it's time to break it all down and make it easy for you to use, review, and adjust as you need to.

For some of you, using a calendar might be as easy as breathing. Maybe you already have a great system that works for you: either a gigantic wall calendar, or a computerized calendar that syncs to all your devices and sends you reminders for things you need to do and places you need to go.

For the rest of us, there are more choices to make. Not everyone can easily break down a school year into calendar days without freaking out. I hope that the following sections will simplify all of this for those of you who aren't used to planning this way. Just like with the values and methods sections, we're going to start big before moving on to smaller and smaller sections.

One of the first things you need to decide before you can really get your plans set is what kind of calendar system you'll use. Now, I'm not talking about lunar calendars versus Gregorian calendars here (although you might need to consider it, especially if you don't live in a place that uses the Gregorian system). I mean, how will you decide when your school year starts or ends? What days will you teach? What days will be holidays? You can make this as flexible or as detailed as you like.

Depending on where you live and what requirements you need to meet, you can set up your calendar in many different ways. Here are a few options:

1. Use the local school district's calendar.

This works great if you have other kids in school or if you want to make sure you keep to a schedule. If you're doing some sort of online schooling, you'll probably have to stick with their schedule.

2. School year-round.

I know several families that continue to school during summer and the holidays because it's easier to keep a routine that way. If you plan to school year-round, you'll most likely benefit from setting easily recognizable bare minimums (from the section on goals) for those times when you want to ease up but don't want to quit completely.

3. Plan a monthly schedule.

One of my friends who uses the Five in a Row curriculum creates beautiful monthly plans for her units. She often decides which units to use based on the season or time of year. This type of planning works great if you are the type to really dive in to holidays and seasonal changes.

4. Make a weekly plan.

This is my favorite method. I plan a 36-week school year, which is the equivalent of 180 days of schooling (the requirement in some states). In the next section, I'll show you how to use a thirty-six-week plan to break down your curriculum into manageable chunks.

5. Don't set a calendar at all.

If you're unschooling, then I'm all for this option. However, if your values and methods don't strongly point to an unschooling way of life, I encourage you not to go down this route. Set your calendar now, and things will be easier in the middle of the year. Flying by the seat of your pants as your child's only education provider isn't recommended, nor is it fun or easy. Choose this option at your own risk.

Decide which type of schedule will work best for you. Be honest with yourself. I often think about schooling year-round, but I adore the freedom and the sunshine during the summer. We still learn a lot, explore a lot, and read a lot of books, but I'm allergic to anything that resembles schoolwork during July. Usually, I need the break even more than the kids do.

Choose the type of schedule that is realistic for you and your life. If you don't like being tied to a daily set of things to do, then a monthly or weekly plan would be better than a school district's calendar full of half days and vacations and make-up days. If you like being told what to do and when to do it (like many of my friends—this is not a bad thing!), then pick a calendar that will hold you accountable to getting things done. Consider doing this part with another homeschooling friend so you can help each other.

Yearly overview

The first thing to do before you start setting dates is to print out or find a yearly calendar. Ideally, you want one that shows the entire year on one or two pages. Since we're planning for a school year, you might need to have two years visible at once. Sometimes I'll use the calendars that come with the local school district's newsletters, since they've already done most of the work for me. If you don't want to purchase a yearly calendar, you can print them for free at donnayoung.org. Her website is a wonderful resource for homeschoolers, with calendars and planning forms of all kinds. You can also do an Internet search for "yearly calendar" and come up with a myriad of options to print out for this step.

We're going to use this calendar to see all the major events and seasons that will happen during your year. You might feel tempted to use a regular monthly calendar for this step, but I don't recommend it. It works better to be able to see the entire school year as one chunk of time. We'll also be quickly counting through weeks to find starting and ending dates for your year. If you have to flip through a lot of pages in order to do this, you might get paper cuts. You can't say I didn't warn you.

With this yearly calendar in hand, circle all the major holidays you celebrate or want to remember, along with birthdays, anniversaries, and any other important events. I usually include bank holidays, not because I celebrate all of them, but because I want to know when things might be busy in my community. When I'm going through this step, I usually include Labor Day, the first day of autumn, Halloween, Thanksgiving, Winter Solstice, Christmas, New Year's, Valentine's Day, St. Patrick's Day, the first day of spring, Passover, Easter, the school district's spring break (so I know when not to take mine), President's Day, and Memorial Day. I'm sure you'll have different holidays, but you get the idea. Any day that might disrupt your normal school day, or for which you might want to do something special, needs to be marked now.

Next, decide which of those holidays will interfere with school and which can be integrated into your studies. Christmas and the New Year usually mean two full weeks off for us. I often take the week of Thanksgiving off due to preparation and travels. Our family used to go to an annual conference in early March. Most of the time, I still counted that week as a full school week because of the different educational experience the kids received there, but sometimes I counted it as a week off. If you're counting a special travel or holiday week as a school week, you might need to rearrange other school subjects around it. This is what you want to note here. If you're planning a thirty-six-week school year, but you're counting a travel week or two, you ultimately get thirty-five weeks (or less) to get through your chosen curriculum for the year.

Most small holidays like Valentine's Day and the bank holidays can be integrated into a week's plans without much disturbance. We might choose to take that day off, to theme our school day around it, or not to celebrate in any major way at all.

For any weeks that I know we will not be doing school, I will draw a line through the entire week on my calendar. This helps me see right away that I won't be planning anything there.

If there are other events you know about that might change the way you plan your year, make sure you have them marked on your schedule. My husband travels to a dozen different conventions each year as part of his job. These dates are all underlined on my yearly calendar so I can see when he'll be gone. They don't change our school weeks very much, but they help me see when he will have long stretches of time at home. He enjoys taking day trips with us, so I often plan trips to zoos or museums when he is in town. I mark all of his trips on my calendar as early as I can so I can adjust our school schedule to fit around them.

Blueprint Sketch #30: Create a yearly overview.

> Print a yearly overview calendar or two calendar years if you're planning for a fall-spring school year. Circle any special days or events. Are there any you might be missing? Which dates will disrupt your school plans? Which dates would you like to integrate into your school plans? If you already know of weeks that will be taken as holidays and not counted as school days, draw a line through them on your calendar. Underline or mark anything else that you want to make note of.

Extra-curricular events and activities

In my many conversations with other parents, I have discovered that we all have a rather silly tendency to underestimate the amount of time and energy required for extracurricular activities. It's almost to the point that, if I didn't have a calendar around, I could still tell you what day and month it was based on which of my friends was having a nervous breakdown from being too busy.

Let's stop deluding ourselves, shall we? School takes time, but so do all those wonderful activities our kids are involved in. Sports take time. Art takes time. Plays and musicals and drama events take time. If your child dances in the Nutcracker every year, know that your December is going to be full of messed up routines and driving to and from rehearsals and dance practices. This doesn't have to be as stressful as it is, sometimes. If you know it's going to happen, you can ease up on other things to allow time for it.

Depending on the activities your family participates in, you might have a number of schedules for certain events. You might have dates for belt-testing for your Taekwondo class, you might have ballet rehearsals, or you might have musical instrument recitals. Maybe you have basketball scrimmages, gymnastics tournaments, or football games. Whatever it is, you probably have a sheet of paper or an email somewhere that tells you the dates of these special events. If nothing else, you know what season of the year those events will take place, because they happen every year.

Instead of letting those things disrupt your homeschool routine, let's make them part of your plans.

Blueprint Sketch #31: Gather the extras.

Go, right now, and gather up all the calendars for your extracurricular activities. These include church events, sports events, and any performance arts you and your children participate in. Print out any schedules that are hidden away in emails. Pull out those letters from the ballet studio or your kids' soccer coach.

Did you get them all?

Are you sure you got them all?

Good. You need those for the next part.

Monthly overview

Now that you have all the major events circled on your yearly calendar, and you have all those sports and performance dates out and in front of you, we're going to look more closely at monthly calendars. Most likely, as you circled those dates on the yearly calendar, you thought of things you want to do or places you want to visit on certain dates. Maybe it even helped you see the perfect week to take your much-needed family vacation. Here's the part where you do a bit of brainstorming to decide how to manage your homeschool plans.

For this step, you need monthly calendars. You can use pretty wall calendars with pictures of kittens, plain monthly calendars printed for free from online, or a professional planner that shows you a month at a time. If you can get a planning calendar that covers the months in a school year, great. I know there are many wonderful calendar systems out there that are created especially for homeschoolers. I prefer to be messy about it, so I print my monthly calendars from online and spread them out in front of me where I can see everything all at once. If you work better with computerized calendars or a system on one of your devices, that works too.

You'll also need your notebook, a few sheets of scratch paper, or a document on your computer where you can take some notes.

Blueprint Sketch #32: Mark your months.

On your monthly calendars, mark all those special dates again. Yes, there is a reason we are doing this twice, and half of it has to do with the fact that you're going to forget all of this tomorrow. In all honesty, the yearly plan will help you see things quickly, and the monthly plans will help you organize at a more detailed level.

Your yearly calendar probably only has holidays and birthdays on it. Your monthly calendars should also include all those extracurricular events, tournaments, performances, and games that you need to attend. You did gather all of these during the last step, right?

This might seem excessive, but I hope you'll see the pay-off when we move on to working out weekly plans. If we manage this part right, your friends will have no idea that it's December, because you won't be freaking out about Nutcracker rehearsals—they'll just be part of your plans for that time. You might even remember to invite your friends early enough that they can purchase tickets before the show sells out.

Brainstorm

Now that you have all your major dates, holidays, and events sketched out on your monthly calendars, you're going to take a few minutes to brainstorm. No matter how complete you were with all those schedules and events, there's something else you do every year that you haven't thought about yet. That's what we're going to find right now.

Take your notebook, several sheets of scratch paper, or a document on your computer. On each page, write the name of a month you'll be including in your school year. I usually teach from mid-August to early June, so I make pages for each of those months.

On each page, make a short list of the activities or events that will happen during that month. Then, make a list of ideas you have for other activities or events you want to do during that month.

Since your major events are marked on your calendars already, you should be able to see your whole month at a glance pretty easily.

Now, quickly list out any ideas you have about things to do during that month.

For example, October is usually an active month for us. Not only are the kids big fans of Halloween, but it's also my son's birthday and the end of the harvest season. It's time to visit the pumpkin patch, clear out the garden, and prepare for winter.

When I'm brainstorming my plans, my notebook page might look like this:

October

 -James's birthday — party?

 -Halloween — costumes? Outlet event - 4pm

 -Pumpkin patch visit

 -Winterize the garden

 -Plant garlic

 -Spider web art

 -carving pumpkins

 -harvest festival

 -learn about harvest traditions in other cultures

 -day of the dead

It takes about five or ten minutes to jot down whatever comes to mind. You don't need to think too hard about it. You should be able to brainstorm your entire year in about twenty to thirty minutes. These are notes to help remind you of the things that might need your time apart from standard school curriculum. As you solidify your curriculum plans, you'll be able to use these notes to see what to integrate into your other activities that month.

Do that for each month. You might have some months without a lot of ideas. For instance, my January list usually looks like this:

January

 -flu season

 -winter

January is either a month spent fighting illness or it's prime school time with very few distractions.

Blueprint Sketch #33: Brainstorm monthly/seasonal events.

> For each month of the year, make a short list. What days are important to you? What do you want to make time to celebrate or prepare for? What community events or family events will happen during the month? If you haven't already,

mark those on your monthly calendar. As we continue planning, keep those monthly lists handy so you can refer to them.

Blueprint Sketch #34: Make notes for planning/prep time.

Of those big events you've sketched out on your monthly plans, do you see any things that will need to be prepared earlier? For instance, every year, I swear I'm going to do an Advent calendar, but by the time the first of December comes charging through my door, I'm still hoarding the last of my Halloween candy and wondering where November went. Instead of December, preparations for that Advent calendar should come in November (if I am going to make or buy one). Make a note to yourself on your monthly calendar for any large event that is going to require extra prep time before it happens.

36-week overview

At this point, your yearly and monthly calendars are probably quite marked up. If you've been following along, you already have recurring yearly events, holidays, and family days circled so they are easy to see. You have all your tournament and performance schedules marked on your monthly calendars, and you've done some brainstorming to see what other events you want to do during each month of the year.

Now that you've done all that, you probably have a much better idea about when you'll need time off from rigorous schooling and when you have weeks that you can devote to bigger school projects. It's also very possible that you've decided that some event or activity is going to be a major time suck and you need to cut it out of your schedule. Good. Let's keep going. We're going to start fitting in those school days, one week at a time.

In the do-it-yourself curriculum section, I talked about the ease of breaking your curriculum into weekly plans. My entire school year is built on this concept. I would go crazy trying to figure out how to plan 180 days of school like most states require. I wouldn't be able to tell you how much work would need to be done each day in order to complete a curriculum in that time. Instead, I can divide it into thirty-six weekly sections, or chunks of six-week long units. This gives me a better idea of how much work will be required to get through a particular curriculum, and whether or not it will be manageable for me and my children.

I've already talked a little bit about why I plan for thirty-six weeks of school every year. Teaching for 5 days a week over 36 weeks equals 180 days of schooling, which is the standard requirement in most states. Using the idea of weekly plans instead of daily, I can easily plan breaks. I like to do school for six weeks on and one week off. Six weeks of school at a time feels manageable, and we always have a good break to look forward to. The weeks off give me a chance to catch my breath, review, and revise my plans as needed.

You don't have to love the thirty-six-week system like I do in order to follow along with the next part. If you're using another calendar system and you want to figure out how to make weekly plans, you'll want to count out the number of full or almost full weeks during which you'll be doing school. You might actually discover you're doing thirty-six weeks without even thinking about it.

Most of the calendar planning section will be built around the idea of using thirty-six weeks for planning. Whether you choose to adopt this system or adapt it for your own needs, I hope that you'll find some tips or tricks to help you manage your yearly plans.

Find a start date

One of the first things you need to do if you're planning your own calendar is to figure out your start date for your school year. Once you have a start date, you can count through the weeks of school to find your target end date. This gives you a good goal to reach for, and makes it easy to see where each of those school weeks will coincide with events on your calendar.

If you're working with a pre-planned calendar and you already know the date you plan to start your year, feel free to pencil it in on your yearly calendar.

If I don't know my start date, and I want to come up with one, I often start out by finding Christmas on my calendar. I assume this will be halfway through my school year, give or take a few weeks. If I can make it through eighteen weeks of school before Christmas, I'll be doing pretty well (or so I reason). I usually start with Christmas because it coincides with a large two-week long break in our year. You can go with whatever major holiday you celebrate, or just start at the New Year. Using my yearly calendar, I count the weeks backwards from Christmas, starting with the week just before. I'm counting all the weeks I plan to do school, so I skip any weeks I've crossed off for holidays or vacations. Since I plan to take a break between every six weeks of schooling, I also skip a week after counting any six weeks together. I count out eighteen weeks of school, plus the breaks, and see where I end up. Quite often, I'm pointing to some date in the middle of July.

At this point, I decide I don't want to start school in July and skip forward to a date in mid-August or early September when I do want to start. I'll count the weeks again and see how many that gets me before Christmas break. I think you get the picture that it's not an exact science, but it's nice to get an idea of how those weeks might fit before you start nailing them down.

If I'm really having trouble deciding when to start, I often ask when others in my homeschool community will be starting their school years. This year, after struggling through the counting of weeks and not being able to decide what to do, I decided to start on the same day as the local school district. Considering that most of the neighborhood kids would be going to back to school on that day and wouldn't be around to play with my kids, that day seemed as good a day as any.

Find the date you want to start. Once we have that start date, we can plan a lot more.

Blueprint Sketch #35: Find your start date.

> Using whatever magical algorithm or star chart you need, find the date on which you want to start your school year. Draw a big circle around it on your yearly calendar. Once we have this date, the rest of it gets easier.

Finding your thirty-six weeks

Now that you have a start date, we're going to find out where your thirty-six weeks of school are going to fit in your year. If you are using a different form of calendar, or already know your start and end dates, feel free to go with what you have planned and skip this step. If you have no idea when you'll be doing school, read on.

Since we're going to go with thirty-six weeks of schooling, we need to do a little counting. We might also need to do some rearranging. I recommend using a pencil for this part.

From your start date, pencil in week numbers on your yearly calendar. I usually write small numbers down the sides of the weeks. Skip any weeks you will be taking off. Add extra break weeks when you will need them. Notice weeks that might be lighter on school and heavy on life. That's normal. We'll roll with those variables in the next step.

After you've numbered out thirty-six weeks, plus any breaks, you'll have a good target end date for your year. Remember how I said to use pencil on those week numbers? If you have just ended your thirty-six-week school year sometime in the middle of July, you might want to make some adjustments. You might decide to move a break to a different week, or not take any breaks at all during a certain period. You might decide you want to do school during the week of Thanksgiving so you don't have to do school in the middle of June. You may decide to start later in September to enjoy (or stay away from) the weather. You might decide to start earlier if it means more flexibility during the winter months. Unless you have a reason to be stuck with the local school calendar, it's really up to you to choose when and how you will manage your school days.

The reason we are trying to get it nailed down now is because it will help you know how much to plan for each of those weeks of your school year. If week 24 is going to land right smack in the middle of three different family birthdays, you're not going to want to plan a multimedia report on World War II, 16 pages of a difficult new math concept, and a day-long science co-op in which you teach cell division to a group of 2nd graders. That may sound outlandish, but it's not far from some of the weeks I've experienced.

I know it may seem crazy to try to figure this all out now. You'll have to make adjustments for illnesses and interruptions, of course. Your plans will change as you go. However, you don't want to ignore the power of making plans just because you're holding your breath for possibilities. Unless you really love waiting and being surprised, there are a lot of things you can prepare for long before they happen.

Blueprint Sketch #36: Sketch out your thirty-six weeks.

Using a pencil, number out all thirty-six weeks on your yearly calendar. Adjust as necessary so you can get the start and end dates you want. Remember, the end goal is to have 180 days on your calendar in an easy-to-use weekly format. You should have a start date, a target end date, and several weeks for breaks marked out. While we will try to keep the schedule fairly flexible, you should have target dates for each of your thirty-six weeks before moving on to the next part. In the next section, we'll work with each of those weeks individually.

If you don't want to use a thirty-six-week system, just make sure you know which days you will be planning on doing school, so we can make some plans and adjustments in the next section. I'd recommend numbering out the school weeks you do have planned, even if they are partial weeks, so you can do the next step in planning.

Weekly calendar

Now that you have your weeks outlined on your yearly calendar and events brainstormed for your school months, it's time to zoom in on your weeks. This is where the real magic happens. On this level, you're finally making plans that you can put into play. You're almost done!

In the next steps, you're going to start plugging curriculum plans in to your school weeks and see how they fit. First, you need to take one final look at your yearly and monthly calendars to see what you need to work around.

For this step, I use an entire sheet of paper in my notebook for each of my school weeks. As I move on to breaking up my curriculum and getting my plans settled, I write my plans onto these sheets. For curricula I've created myself, I print out my weekly plans, cut them apart, and then tape them on these weekly planning sheets. It looks terrible but works beautifully for me. Since the thirty-six-week breakdown can feel like such a modular system, it's easy to shift subjects around in weekly blocks in my notebook. If I could find a computer program that let me plan in weekly blocks rather than imprisoning me in a daily timed schedule, I would be a happy homeschooler. All of the planning programs I have used lock me into daily plans, which I'm not fond of.

You don't have to do your weekly sheets the same way I do. What you want is a way to see each of your weeks at a glance, in the same way we've seen your entire year and each of your months individually. You could use index cards. You could use scratch paper. You could use the weekly portion of your planner if you have one.

You'll want to have one sheet of paper or index card for each of your thirty-six weeks (or the number of school weeks you're planning for, based on the calendar you built in the last step). On each piece of paper, write the number of the week and the dates of that week in your school year as found on your yearly calendar. Underneath, note any special events that are happening during that week. We're not messing with recurring events yet. If you have ballet every Wednesday night at 5:30, it doesn't go here. This is for the events or activities you'll be doing that will be out of your normal routine.

If absolutely nothing is happening during that week, don't write anything. Heave a sigh of relief.

As we move forward into breaking up your curriculum plans, these notes will help you see where you might have distractions or interruptions that will alter your school schedule. They'll also help you come up with other ideas for activities to integrate into your schooling that week.

Blueprint Sketch #37: Make your weekly notes.

Take out your notebook, weekly planner, or a stack of scratch paper or index cards. If you're sticking to the thirty-six-week system, you'll need thirty-six separate sheets or sections.

On each card or section of your paper, write the number of the week and the dates on your calendar where that week is penciled in. Underneath, write any events that will happen during that week. Since you already circled most of this on your yearly and monthly plans, this should be pretty easy. Note if you need to prepare for something that is coming up the following week.

Once you're done with this step, you have the full skeleton of your homeschool year. You've started building that awesome house you've been dreaming of. The foundation is poured, the walls are standing, and the roof is on. It's all coming together now. All we need to do next is put up some sheetrock and get the electrical wired, and then it's time to decorate and move in.

Weekly overview and curriculum breakdown

In Part Four, I gave you some ideas for finding your curriculum for the year. I also talked about creating your own curriculum if you couldn't find what you were looking for. During this step, you're going to break down all those curriculum plans into weekly chunks, and then plug them in to your calendar and see how they fit. This part combines those weekly goals you set back in Part Three with your actual calendar plans to help you create the optimal plan for that week of your school year. This can be as simple or as complicated as you want it to be.

The first thing we're going to do is create a weekly overview plan. This is going to be one single sheet that shows you everything you need to get through during any given week, from each of your different subjects. How do you know what to get through each week?

Remember those daily goals you set back in Part Three? These were the lists of subjects you planned to cover on each day of your school week. Using that list as your guide, you're going to break up your curriculum into thirty-six weeks of plans to see what will be required each week.

Depending on the subject you're working on and the type of curriculum you have, there are several different ways to break things up.

1. Number of Pages

First, you can break your curriculum into the number of pages you need to complete each week. For any curriculum that you want to get through this year that requires you to simply do one page after another, this is the easiest option. It requires a bit of math and possibly some adjustment as you look at units and lessons.

With your curriculum in hand, figure out how many pages of text you will work through during the year. The easiest way to do this is to see how many pages are in the book. If you want to be more technical about it, count all the pages in the book that you will actually work on.

Now that you know the total number of pages to work through, divide that number by the number of weeks you will be doing school. If you are using the 36-week system, and you have 280 pages in your textbook, you will divide 280 into 36 equal parts. A calculator might be useful, unless you have a child in the house who needs some long division practice. After doing the calculations, I see that 280 pages divided by 36 weeks would come out to around 7.8 pages per week. Round up for flexibility, and you know you have to cover about 8 pages a week of that curriculum in order to finish by the end of your school year.

2. Units or Lessons

Some curricula are broken into lessons or chapters that don't make sense to cut into page numbers. If the curriculum you're looking at is like this, then you'll want to break it into chunks that you can manage on a weekly or monthly level. If your curriculum includes forty-two lessons, you may want to decide now what lessons to combine or cut out in order to finish the entire thing in thirty-six weeks or less.

If you need to break your curriculum into chunks or unit topics, you might want to reference the Do-It-Yourself History section in Part Four for a detailed example of how I do this. I imagine many science curricula would fall under this type of breakdown, where you want to keep certain topics together, rather than simply require a number of pages. By the time you finish this step, you'll have a list of topics that you'll be covering for each week of your year.

3. Practice Time or Session Requirements

If you're working through any mastery-based program, it may not be feasible to set a yearly goal to finish it, or it may be difficult to break up into weekly requirements because you're not sure how much must be done in order to finish. There might be times when learning a new skill takes more time and looks like fewer pages or units of work. If you're working through a curriculum that requires practice time instead of page numbers, feel free to break that down as you see fit.

Some examples of curricula that would require practice time might include Sequential Spelling, foreign languages, and reading programs. Musical instrument practice and online lessons might be broken up this way as well.

You might be rolling your eyes at the thought of breaking out every single one of your subjects this way. Don't worry. You don't have to do it for everything. For many subjects, I practically phone this in. For instance, I know I want to do Sequential Spelling twice a week with my kids. Yes, I know that program calls for daily practice. No, it doesn't fit into my schedule that way. Because of that, I know we're not going to make it through an entire level each year of school. Thankfully, it's a flexible enough program that it's not restricted to particular grade levels.

Since it's a sequential program, it needs to be done in a particular order, one step at a time. That makes the planning pretty simple. I don't set a goal to make it through a whole book in a year. I just plan to get to it twice a week. All I need to manage that is a bookmark and a note to myself to teach it on particular days. I do the same with Latin, the Daily Language Review I use, and the Critical Thinking book we're working through.

If you need specific examples of each of the ways of breaking things down, here are the different ways I've broken up math over the years.

At first, I used a fairly traditional curriculum written for homeschoolers called Math Mammoth. I adored Math Mammoth so much that I bought the entire elementary set, first through sixth grade, in one large bundle. I planned to use it for all of those years, too, but only made it through fourth grade before I needed to make some revisions in my plans.

Math Mammoth includes the teaching text and the worksheets together in a single printable curriculum. For each year that I was planning math, I would simply look at the number of pages in each of those years of curriculum, divide by 36, and come up with the number of pages the child would have to finish in order to make it through the whole curriculum in one year.

Math Mammoth Grade Three includes two student worktexts. The first one is 184 pages long. The second one is 177 pages long. Added together, that's 361 sheets of worktext to cover in one year. Divide that by 36, and the result is just over 10. Ten pages of math each week really isn't much. That's only two pages of math a day, if I teach math five days a week. That's not too bad. At this point, I would write down the weekly requirements for math, print it all out if I wanted to, and consider it done.

As my daughter grew older, I noticed she had a lot of trouble with the more traditional ways of learning math. She is a kinesthetic learner, and has always learned far more from playing with things like Cuisenaire rods, dominoes, dice, math balances, and geoboards. As she struggled through all of first grade in Math Mammoth, I realized I was working twice as hard to teach her with that curriculum, since I had to translate it all into stories and objects that she could play around with. After a year of it, I decided it was time to move her into a different program.

For a while, I couldn't find a curriculum that I thought would work for her. Everyone recommended Math-U-See, but that still felt too structured and was outside of our budget. I decided to modify the Math Mammoth plans instead, and do math in a series of units and topic studies. I looked through the major topics in Math Mammoth for second grade, which included hundreds charts, reading a clock and a calendar, addition and subtraction with regrouping over ten, geometry, simple fractions, money, and beginning multiplication. Using those topics as unit ideas, I worked with her with the manipulatives we had around the house until she mastered each idea. When I planned for that year, I wrote the main math topic and a few ideas or resources to use as my plan for the week.

Then, I discovered Khan Academy. To say that Khan Academy changed my life might be a bit of a stretch, but only a bit. Everyone in the family now has an account on Khan Academy, where we continue to learn new concepts, take quizzes on the old, and earn badges and rewards for mastering challenges. I have one overriding goal for each child on Khan Academy: by the end of the year, they should achieve 100% mastery of their grade level on the site.

Since the site tracks your mastery percentage in such a visible way, this becomes a fun game for them. I try hard to stay ahead of both of them, too, which helps me teach any concepts that they struggle with in their grade level. As their coach on the site, I can recommend activities for them to practice based on where they are. I've already mastered everything the kids are currently learning, so I can easily help them with it. I often sit with my daughter as she works through new concepts and talk her through it until she is confident enough to send me away. My son likes to watch the videos to learn new ways of calculating things.

Since there's no real way to know how quickly they will master a grade, I set a daily minimum for each of the kids: complete three activities on Khan Academy each day. That might include one mastery challenge and two practice challenges, or it might be all mastery challenges or all practice levels. Often, they'll get going and won't stop at three activities. Even with a minimum of three a day, I notice they are well on their way to achieving mastery in their current grade levels.

Those are examples of how I've had to break up math in three different ways over the year. Depending on the curriculum you're using, and your preferred method of teaching and record-keeping, you might choose to break up your subjects any number of ways. The important thing is to break it up so you have realistic expectations for each week.

Blueprint Sketch #38: Break it down.

Using the list of weekly goals you made in Part Three, break down each of those subjects you will be teaching during your school year. How much will you have to cover in each subject each week in order to meet your goals by the end of the year? Break up each of your curriculum choices into page numbers, unit topics, or practice times.

How much weekly practice will be required? If you split your curriculum into unit topics, do you have a chosen unit for each of your thirty-six weeks of school plans?

List your supply needs

Some of your curriculum is going to require special supplies. If you're doing any sort of science experiment, art project, game, or hands-on practice, you will need supplies.

If you've been homeschooling for any amount of time, you know what it feels like to be missing those supplies when you need them. Unless you're already pretty well organized, or you're just downright stingy about your materials, stuff gets used and lost all the time. I reorganize my school supplies every summer, and usually find all my precious things again, hidden away in places they didn't belong. It's kind of exciting, though. It's like having a used curriculum sale where I want to buy everything and discover that it's already all mine.

It used to be much worse, until I started planning my weeks clearly. Now, when it comes time to sit down and perform a particular science experiment, I am usually on top of things. Thanks to my weekly breakdown, I know exactly what's coming up in my plans and I know what supplies I need. I can gather or purchase any materials I need and put them in a place where I will actually find them when it comes time to do that project.

If you would like to have the same peace of mind, it's not too difficult a task. It does require looking through your full year of chosen curriculum or self-made plans and making lists of each of the things you'll need each week for hands-on projects.

For a pre-made curriculum, this is often quite easy—especially if it comes with a kit of materials already pulled out for you. For a curriculum that brags about using "common household objects," I'm afraid you'll have to do a bit of work. I often find those books assume I have things like borax, plaster of Paris, and a drawer full of balloons just sitting around in my house. I don't. Well, I do now, but I didn't before I started.

For any curriculum that has hands-on projects, you can add one extra step to make your plans even more detailed. Go through your curriculum, one week at a time, and make a note of any of the projects you'll be doing. What resources will you need to do those projects?

Sometimes, these things do seem like they will be easy-to-find materials. If the project calls for construction paper and oil pastels, you might assume that you'll have them on hand when the time comes. Don't underestimate the power of children to anticipate your upcoming needs. We could go an entire year without ever touching our stock of modeling clay, but if I have an art project on the horizon in a few weeks that requires clay, you can bet my kids will have a sudden and uncontrollable urge to play with clay. If I didn't already have notes about my plans, I might forget until I need that clay. Instead, I remember that I need it and keep enough of it for our project and let the kids take the rest for their endeavors.

Before you move forward, make supply lists for each week for any of your subjects that need them. If you need to check out extra books from the library, buy oil pastels, or make sure you have Epsom salts on hand for that science experiment, make a list now.

I prefer to do this in a separate document from my weekly plans, so I can shift them around as necessary. I will make a new document for art or science supplies, and put the week number, the name of the project, and the list of needed supplies. When I'm done, I print these out, cut them up, and then stick them into my weekly plans where they'll fit best. You might just want to write them directly into your weekly plans. Whatever works best for you.

Blueprint Sketch #39: Make curriculum supply lists.

Go through any of your books and textbooks that will require additional supplies. Try not to assume that you will have everything you need. Make a list for each week of the things you'll need for that particular curriculum. Once your plans are put together, it will be very easy to gather everything you need for a week's worth of schooling.

As you find things you don't already own, add them to your shopping list. I'm usually able to buy all my supplies for science and art at a discount during the summer. The hardest part is keeping those supplies organized and unused until the time we need them for school. Sometimes, I'll have to restock my stash during the middle of the year.

Weekly plans

My weekly plans can be a squirrely bunch. Trying to nail them down ahead of time can often be a challenging ordeal. However, once they are set, I find that they are the easiest things in the world to manage.

In the last step, you broke your entire curriculum into thirty-six weekly pieces and made a master list of everything you would cover in any given week of school. I imagine most of your curriculum was easy to break up into page numbers or practice times. It's going to be easy to keep up with that once you get started.

For any curriculum that you split into units, you'll want to keep track of what units you'll be covering and when. This is where those weekly calendars you made come in handy. For any subject that has a different topic or idea to study each week, you want to make a note of it on the corresponding weekly calendar.

There are a few different ways to do this. Feel free to be creative with the way you manage your plans. I've tried note cards and spreadsheets, and have currently resorted to paper, pens, computer printouts, and tape. What I really care about is that my weekly plans are easy to see at a glance, easy to adjust while I'm planning, and easy to use when I need to reference them.

When I create my own curricula for history and science, I type up my final plans with week numbers and book and resource lists. When those plans are done, I print them out and then cut them into blocks. Each of those blocks is a single week's worth of school plans for that particular subject, complete with book lists. Once I have those blocks cut out, I tape them, one by one, into my notebook.

Here's where this step has a magical payoff.

Because you've already set the dates of each of your weeks, and you know what events are happening during each week, you can see whether or not your chosen units will work well in any given week. Some units are easy. Some are more involved. Some weeks are full before you ever come to schooling. Some weeks are so wide open you could launch a rocket from them.

You might have a huge unit planned for science during one week, and you start to write your history plans and see that history is going to be very time-consuming as well. You might see that you're planning to cover Greece in Geography, but it's St. Patrick's Day, so it might be a better week to cover Ireland instead. You might have organized a set of units around picture books and realize that one will be perfect to supplement your planned trip to the pumpkin patch.

These weeks are still completely customizable at this point, and depending on how you finalize them and set them up, they could be customizable for the entire year. You should be able to look at any subject plan during any given week and think, "That's not going to work" and switch it out with the thing that will.

This part can look a lot like putting together a giant jigsaw puzzle. Depending on how much is pre-planned for you and how much you plan for yourself, you might have a lot to figure out here. You might completely hate this part. I enjoy the challenge, but since I create much of my own curriculum, a lot of this falls into place when I'm setting up each of my subjects.

At the same time, don't try to make this complicated if it doesn't seem to be complicated for you. I just looked through my notebook and found a week that has exactly two items on it: a history video to watch and a science book to check out. I kept it simple because I knew we would be coming off a difficult set of weeks and would need a rest. Because the majority of my other subjects are pre-planned or require practice time rather than topic studies, that week pretty much planned itself.

Blueprint Sketch #40: Put together the puzzle.

For any of your school subjects that have varying topic lists or units, note these on your weekly calendars. Rearrange things as necessary. If your topics can be taught in any order, move topics to weeks that contain events that will correspond better to the ideas you're teaching. Skip weeks that are already heavy with other activities or subjects. Combine topics that will be covered during your week via other subjects or activities.

Blueprint Sketch #41: Make extra notes.

Once you've added your subjects to your weekly plans, take a minute to look them over. Are there any extra projects you'd like to do for those topics? Do you want to find library books on any particular subjects? Are there any field trips you could take during that week? Do you want to talk to your homeschool group about doing a co-op on any of your subjects during certain weeks? Are there any extra items you need to pick up to manage your projects or experiments for that week?

Note those now. As you prepare for your school weeks, you'll be able to see those notes on your weekly plans and take action on them. If there is anything that needs to be added to your monthly calendar, feel free to add it now.

Daily plans

What about daily plans?

To be honest, I never go much further than weekly plans when I'm breaking up my curriculum for the school year. Back in the goals section, you created a list for each day of the week to detail when you would teach certain subjects. At this point, I review that list, adjust any subjects that I added or got rid of, and add notes for any extracurricular activities that happen on the same day each week. This is as far as I ever go with it. I don't try to nail each page of my curriculum to a certain day in a calendar. Part of this is because I really like to maintain an image of flexibility. My plans really aren't that flexible, but they feel more flexible this way. Sure, I'm teaching history two days a week, and I know that I'm teaching about the Indus Valley next week, but there is no way you can get me to commit to reading pages 14 through 19 of my history encyclopedia at 10 a.m. next Monday. I know I'm kidding no one here. It's going to happen. I just hate getting stuck that tightly to a schedule.

Today is a Tuesday. Today, according to my weekly plans, I should have taught Math, Daily Language, Reading, Fitness, Science, Handwriting, and Getting Started with Latin. I didn't. My husband had the day off. The kids woke up with ideas for computer programming and art that they wanted to do. Instead of pushing for a regular day, I swapped out my Tuesday plans for my Wednesday plans: art, critical thinking, and learning/computer games. After a relaxing morning of "fun" school, we went to the beach. It was the perfect day for it. The kids still learned a lot, and our art project was a great success.

When it comes time to do school tomorrow, I just have to pull out my Tuesday list and move through those subjects. No bother. No frantic feeling of being behind or failing today. That's half the reason I schedule a floater day of art, logic, and educational games.

The other thing is that once my weekly plans are set and my daily subjects are listed in a way I can reference, this whole machine works on its own. I get up in the morning, have a cup of tea so I can figure out what day it is, and then check the day's schedule. I write the things we'll study on the school white board, where everyone can see it. Depending on what's happening that day, I might skip a subject or add one. Then we go through the day, completing each task and crossing them off. We don't always do them in a particular order. Every day is a little different than the day before, and that's okay for me. It also works for my kids.

We do have daily goals for particular subjects. Reading is for thirty minutes a day. Math includes three exercises on Khan Academy. Daily Language is a page of writing and editing each day. However, if I had to put all of these things into 180 individual days of scheduling, I would rebel. I would kick and scream and pull my hair and decide that homeschooling was too hard and you couldn't make me do it.

The irony is that with my weekly plans and my daily subject lists, I have pretty much tricked myself into creating 180 days of plans. I just don't think of it that way.

If you feel like you need to create more specific daily plans and put them on your calendar, feel free. I know there are a lot of people who work better with very specific daily plans. For any weekly goals, you can simply divide by the number of days you'll teach that subject each week to get a daily number of pages to cover.

There are many planning programs available where you can input these plans and get daily lists of assignments for any given day. If you like having daily plans scheduled out for you, you might want to look into one of the planners like Homeschool Skedtrack or Homeschool Planet. I hope that all this work on goals and plans down to the weekly level will help you create your daily schedules the way you want them.

Blueprint Sketch #42: Revise your daily list.

> Take one last glance through the daily subject lists you made in Part Three. Do you still want to cover those subjects on those days of the week? Do you have recurring activities like music or athletics on certain days of the week that you can add to your lists?

If you want to manage your curriculum on a more specific daily level, feel free to take some time to nail down your page numbers and topic ideas for each day of your school year.

Finalizing the weeklies

Once you have your weekly plans sorted out and in place, you're basically done. Depending on how nice you want things to look, you might want to take one extra step here and type everything up into a set of final plans.

I keep a spreadsheet in Google Drive that shows me all my major topics and courses of study at a glance. I print it out on a single sheet and put it in the front of my homeschool binder, so I can always see what my plans are. This spreadsheet does not contain my book and resource lists, though. It only gives me an overview of what we're studying and not the details. At this time, my planning notebook full of doodles, lists, and taped-in history and science plans is the notebook I work from at the weekly level. I printed out my art plans for the year and put them in my teaching binder. I know I just need to do the next one each week. The rest of my curriculum books and the kids' workbooks have bookmarks in them to mark our place and they all sit together in one section of our homeschool shelves.

In past years, I have typed up all my weekly plans, including topic headers, book lists, art projects, science experiment supplies, musician studies, Latin words, and way too many other things into rather lovely documents. This year, I decided it would take too much time and energy to create a final document, so I didn't. Sometimes it helps to have something that looks nice to work from. Sometimes it doesn't matter. You have to decide what will work better and make better sense for you.

If this entire process has been done on scraps of paper that are now strewn all throughout your entire house, I highly recommend getting a folder or binder to organize those things in case you want to reference them later. What you really want to have now is an easy-to-find and easy-to-use reference that tells you exactly what you need and when.

There are a number of things that you've created that you will want to keep within reach during your homeschool year.

First, you decided on your homeschool values and chose a saying or quote to help keep those values visible for you during your year.

Second, you made a set of weekly subject goals that make sense for you and your family. You split these weekly goals into five daily lists including the subjects or ideas you would be covering during each day of the week. This also included your recurring activities and practices.

Third, you decided what your "bare minimums" would be, should anything disrupt your homeschool year. Don't hesitate to look at these and resort to them when you need to. You may just need one day. You may need a month. Just remember that you have them and that they are there to help you manage.

Fourth, we set a master-list of weekly goals: pages of curriculum to complete, particular topics or units to cover, or goals for practice sessions or time needed in a subject. This gives you a goal to shoot for each week so you know you're staying on track with those ideals of finishing curriculum levels by the end of your year.

Fifth, we set up individual weeks of plans, adjusted to fit in your family's yearly calendar, that cover any special topics, activities, or ideas that you want to cover during the weeks of your school year.

If you don't already have these things together in one place, let's organize them.

Blueprint Sketch #43: Finalize your documents.

Decide how you will file the plans you just finished. Will you type everything into a set of beautiful documents on your computer? Will you copy it all into a pretty planner or journal? Will you keep it all in the dog-eared, coffee-stained notebook where it is? Will you sort it into a nice homeschool binder, where it's easy to see and use?

Everything on my computer is sorted into a homeschool planning folder so I can easily find it and reference it when I need to. Everything that is printed or written on is stored in my teaching binder, which acts as my brain during my year.

Get all your plans in a final order now. Keep in mind that your final order might change. Just like with teaching styles and curriculum choices, you might end up changing the way you manage your plans. You might decide that loose leaf paper works better for you. You might want to get your major documents laminated so you can cross them off each week as you go and reuse them over and over. Just get them into a form that you can use as you start your year.

Calendar review

You've made it through and your yearly plans are done! Congratulations! Now you just need to get them rolling and keep them maintained during your year. Part Six will give you some of my favorite tips for keeping a homeschool year running smoothly once you've started it.

Here are the calendar tasks to review.

~ Decide what calendar planning system you will use for your school year. Will you plan your days alongside the local school district? Will you school year-round? Will you make monthly or weekly plans?

~ Print out a yearly calendar or two that will show you your entire school year at a glance. Circle all the holidays and special events. Draw a line through weeks you plan to take off from school. Underline any other events you want to remember that might change your school plans.

~ Print out or find monthly calendars that cover your school year. Mark all your special events and extracurricular events on your monthly calendars. Take a moment to brainstorm any activities or ideas you have about things to do during each month of your school year.

~ Find your start date and end date for your school year. Make sure you've planned enough days to stay within your local requirements if you have to keep attendance records.

~ Count out the number of weeks that you'll be schooling during the year to make your curriculum plans easier. If you're planning on schooling for thirty-six weeks, number your thirty-six weeks on your yearly calendar so you can clearly see them.

~ Make or find a calendar for each of your school weeks. Mark out the dates, and make a note of any events or activities that are happening during those weeks.

~ Break each of your curriculum choices into thirty-six weekly chunks. Make a master list of weekly goals that tells you exactly how much of each workbook, text, or curriculum to finish each week so you can finish by the end of the year.

~ For any of your curriculum choices that need to be split into units, split them into thirty-six pieces or fewer. Put these idea blocks on your weekly calendars, and rearrange them until they make sense for your schedule.

~ Cut things out into daily plans if you need to.

~ Finalize your plans and gather them all into one place so you can easily reference them when you need them.

Part Six: Making It Work

Preparing for the year

Now you have plans. Hooray! Congratulations on making it through all those steps. But what in the world are you going to do with those plans? Are you going to file them away, forget about them and just move on at your usual frantic pace? I hope not.

There are three steps to managing your plans now, all of which will be ongoing through your year.

First, you need to prepare. During the planning process, you took a lot of notes and found a lot of resources. In order to follow through with the plans you made, you need to keep looking ahead to make sure you have what you want or need for your upcoming weeks. You'll need to request things from the library, buy supplies for your projects, and prepare your home or your family for upcoming activities.

Second, you need to put the plans in play. The best plans in the world aren't worth a thing if you don't actually use them. You'll need to form some good habits to continue managing the plans you have. This can be difficult at first, but it gets easier.

Third, you should review and revise as necessary. Now that you have been through the full planning process once, it's easier to move things around and adjust your schedule when you need to. Review often. Double-check that the plans are working. Revise if necessary.

Prepare

Do you know how driver's manuals always tell you to look several car lengths ahead as you're driving on a highway? In a car, looking ahead keeps you from getting in an accident. In your homeschool year, looking ahead helps you stay on the road.

Now that you've made plans that encompass your entire year, you shouldn't have many surprises at all. Everything is laid out for you, from your event schedules to your family birthdays to the supplies you need for science experiments. You know when your sports tournaments and art performances are going to happen. You also know what you will do if anything major happens to disrupt your normal routine. But knowing is only half the battle, to borrow a phrase from my childhood. The only way these things will work as well as you want them to is if you prepare for them before they happen.

You'll want to manage your preparations on two different levels. First, you'll want to keep those monthly plans handy. On the first of each month, look through the list you made of things to do or prepare for. Are all of those events on your monthly calendar or on your radar, at least? Are there any that you need to purchase tickets for or purchase supplies for?

Second, you want to manage your weekly plans.

In my experience, I've found that it helps to have one day a week to manage plans. I might do this on a Friday evening just after finishing a week of school, or on a Sunday evening as I prepare for the next week. Sometimes it's after two or three cups of tea in the middle of a Wednesday, when I realize everything is really off-kilter and I should definitely figure out what in the world I'm trying to do.

My goal, when I'm actually managing well, is to stay two weeks ahead in my preparations. This gives me wiggle room as I search for any needed supplies, and also ensures I always have the library books I need.

On your weekly plans, you made lists of resources you would need to do your projects and experiments. If you manage your plans two weeks in advance, this gives you plenty of time to purchase or gather those materials so you have them when you need them. You also made notes about upcoming events, holidays, birthdays, and tournaments. Keeping two weeks ahead means you'll see your notes about an upcoming birthday and you'll be able to prepare for it.

If you want to borrow a particular book from the library, the best way to make sure you have it when you need it is to put it on hold with your library system. You can do this through the online catalog or in person with a librarian. Many local libraries have a limited number of books on their shelves. If I walk in on the day I need a book, the odds of me going home with the particular book I have in mind are pretty slim. This is especially true if it's a popular book. Those books rarely sit around on the shelves. In fact, the only way to get some books during the first year or two of their release is to get on the waiting list for a hold. I have been on waiting lists for library books with over a hundred people requesting the book before me.

This is also true around holidays. Have you ever walked into the library during the week of Thanksgiving, hoping to find a few picture books about Thanksgiving? I have. The shelves of holiday books have usually been picked cleaner than a turkey carcass by then. In my experience, most popular holiday books are checked out a week or two in advance of any given holiday. If you want books about particular holidays, you want to make sure you put them on hold several weeks in advance.

If your local library doesn't have a book you want on the shelves, that doesn't mean you can't get it. Most libraries have partnerships with a number of other libraries in the area, and they can easily swap books to ensure you get the book you want. In most cases, this service is totally free. However, because the other libraries are usually in other towns, it may take a while for the books to arrive. It takes my local library anywhere from three to ten days to gather books for me, if there is not a waiting list for any of the books.

I've been told I'm considered a "power user" of my library. In both of the library systems I've used while homeschooling, the librarians knew who I was because I had a rather large chunk of shelving devoted to my holds. I might take home anywhere from ten to fifty books during any given week. This is a fantastic problem for your local library. Since most of them get their funding based on their circulation and the number of books moving through the system, you're doing them a favor by using so many resources. Of course, unless you want to keep funding your library through payment of fines for overdue books, you'll need to make sure you give those books back on time or renew them.

If you just want to check out a number of books on a particular subject, and it's not related to any upcoming holidays or popular events, you may not have to get too involved with the holds system. You can just walk in and browse the books on the shelves when you need them. In that case, you may not need to manage your books two weeks in advance.

Staying two weeks ahead in your preparations can give you a significant boost in your ability to manage your time and supplies. Rather than rushing around at the last minute (which you will probably do anyway, because it happens), you can prepare for upcoming lessons and events. You can also borrow or purchase anything you need so you have it on hand when you need it.

Keeping it rolling during the year

Planning and preparing are always great in theory. It feels great to finish those lovely spreadsheets and fill out those calendars and forms. It's fun to buy supplies and gather books and get ready for upcoming events. Maybe it wasn't that fun for you, but that's my favorite part of the year.

It's the day-to-day stuff that does me in.

You just planned for 180 days of school, split into 36 weeks. That's 180 days of plans you'll have to follow through on. That means you have to get up every single day, teach your major subjects, battle through learning, fight the tears (not just yours, but the kids' tears too), and make this year happen. You have goals for the things you want to finish, and you know how much you need to do each week to make that happen. This is all great, until you realize that learning can be very hard. Homeschooling is a full-time job. You don't exactly get to coast through it. That doesn't mean it's not fun or doesn't come with significant rewards of its own.

How do you manage the day-to-day homeschool routine? Depending on your own methods and preferences, you might need to come up with some tricks to help you. I'll share a few that I use, and maybe they'll help you come up with ways to manage your own days.

1. Visual Reminders

I am a very visual person. I learn best from reading and pictures, and I constantly make lists and notes to help remind myself of things. If it's not in front of my face, it's lost. That's why both my teaching binder and my home planning binder are bright yellow. It's not because yellow is my favorite color. It's because the yellow is such an eyesore that I can always find my binders.

Because I know I'm such a visual person, I make a lot of charts that allow me to see progress. Each of my kids has a 6x6 chart that maps out their 36 weeks of school. At the end of each week, I write the date it was completed, and they can put stickers in the completed weeks if they want to. These charts help everyone see how we're doing. Often, the kids will come to put their stickers on and say, "We finished that much school already?" or "Look, we're halfway there!" It encourages us all to see how far we've come and that there is only a little further to go each school year.

That works on a weekly level. What about on a daily level?

Last year, I started a new habit that works really well for me. I hung a white board in the homeschool area. (Confession: it's my kitchen. I call it a homeschool area because that sounds so much more professional.) Each morning, as I drink my dose of caffeine and try to get my eyes to open enough to pretend I'm alive, I get out the day's list of subjects. I write them all out on the white board, making any modifications for the day that I deem necessary. As the kids work through their subjects, they cross them off or draw stars or grades next to them. (I once happened upon my chart halfway through a school day, where one of my children had written a new subject: "Torture" and next to it was written "Mom" with a huge A+. I look back on that moment with great pride.)

My husband keeps suggesting I use a Sharpie to draw a permanent chart on this whiteboard, but I keep resisting. Some days, I just write messages or draw pictures on there to symbolize our daily subjects. I like being able to write my schedule every day, but I don't like feeling like I absolutely have to write a schedule there every day. And I really love being able to erase things when it becomes obvious that it's a bare minimum day and not a rigorous day full of epiphanies and grand discoveries.

2. Make It a Habit

One of the most common reasons my friends give for schooling year-round is that it's easier to keep the routine this way. There is power in the habit of doing the same or similar things every day. Over time, you start to realize how much time it takes to finish school work during the day, and both you and the kids will become more efficient at it. I also find that the resistance to school work that we all suffer in the beginning is much diminished after a week or two. If you keep a good routine and everyone in the house knows what that routine is, it's harder to break out of it.

The first few weeks of a new school year are always the hardest, at least for me. During that first week, the kids still hold out hope that I'm joking about how much work we'll do. I think I usually hope I'm joking as well, because it means I have to do things. It takes a lot longer for all of us to focus, and subjects that should only take fifteen minutes might take an hour or more. It can be very frustrating.

After a few weeks, things are usually humming right along. The kids know exactly what work they have to do, and I am better about facilitating that for them. Once we've made a habit out of our daily tasks, school is easier for all of us. It's also a lot more fun as we come up with ways to enjoy what we're learning.

We had some busier-than-normal days last week, and by Friday, we were all pretty worn out. I stumbled out to the white board in the morning and wrote all the subjects on the board. I made a face.

"I don't want to," I thought. "Let's just take the day off."

Then I started reasoning with myself: "We have to do the bare minimums anyway, which is math and daily language work. And if we're going to do that, it won't take too much extra to add in the geography and history. Oh, and I remember that the Latin lesson was going to be easy. And since we have new books from the library, reading will be fun today." I shared my reasoning with the kids, and we all decided to go for the full day. I think we were done by noon. Being in the habit of doing school every morning helped us all push through and get it done. It also helped that we went to buy toys later, which leads me to my next tip.

3. Reward Yourself

I don't always believe in rewards systems as motivators for learning, but I am prone to falling back on them quite often. The rewards here are not for my children; they are for me.

Homeschooling can be a thankless job. First of all, you don't get paid for it. Second of all, unless you join a homeschool community, you probably have no adults in your peer group to talk to. Third, you are prone to all sorts of harassment and assaults on your person each and every day, and that's just your children I'm talking about. Depending on the ages of your children, and whether there is a rabid toddler rampaging through your school days, you may consider it a success if you don't get vomited on, told off, sneered at, or have a toy smashed in your face while you're trying to lie down for a minute. Just admit it: you love your children, but it's hard.

Instead of finishing a school day and thinking of all the ways I failed as a parent or an educator, I reward myself for surviving the day. Once school is done for the day, I am off. I play a video game. I read a book. I eat a piece of chocolate. I might only get half an hour before it's time to start dinner and move on to the bedtime routines, but I'm taking it. I need it for my sanity.

I know this isn't always a possibility, and it depends on the ages of your kids as much as anything else. But giving yourself a pat on the back for a job well done can go a long way toward giving you the energy to get up the next morning to do it again.

If you can't take a single moment to yourself, try a mental exercise instead. Think of three different things that went well during your day. Smile, and tell yourself you did a good job. You did! Positive reflection can help you feel better about the day and about homeschooling in general.

4. Take Breaks

Many studies have shown the benefits of recess for a child's well-being and development. Studies of the schools in Finland show that the kids there benefit from having a fifteen-minute break every hour.

I don't know how you run your homeschool day, but I have a tendency to want to get it done in one fell swoop. I know that we could be done by noon every day if we just sat down, shut up, and worked hard. But kids don't work that way. I don't work that way. I usually hit my limit after around forty-five minutes of any difficult activity.

Starting last year, I instituted my own form of recess. After every subject, we take a break of about fifteen minutes. The kids often go outside, usually to gather food for whatever creature we're currently housing as a science experiment. I might make myself a cup of tea and watch the hummingbirds out my window. After a few minutes, we gather up and get back to school, ready to learn and curious about the world again. It's amazing how little time it takes to reset your mind and mood.

I know a lot of homeschool parents who spend their entire day rotating through teaching kids. When one child is on a break, you're with another child. You might spend eight or ten hours a day doing this, forgetting to eat or drink or care for yourself at all. If you do this, you're on the fast track to burn out. Remember that you need a break just as much as the kids do. Be the model of good behavior and self-care for your children, and take breaks throughout your school days.

5. Be a Good Manager

I like to imagine that homeschooling is my job. In terms of time and energy required, it certainly counts as a full-time job. But what I mean is that I try to imagine myself as an employee of a company. Maybe I have a bit of a split personality, because I am also my own manager in this company. I'm also the lunch lady and the evil receptionist, but that's another story. Am I a good manager? This is what I like to ask myself. Do I make myself work overtime and on Saturdays because the work is never done? Or do I let myself go home from work and do something that has nothing to do with my job?

Homeschooling is a lifestyle more than anything else, and as such, you may never get time off. You may be up at midnight answering your child's curious question about the origin of the wedding ring, like I did last week. You may spend a Saturday fielding questions about the nature of the universe and the scientific possibilities to explain black holes. That's homeschooling.

But if you're making extra work for yourself all day long just because you don't feel like you're doing enough, you just might be a tyrannical manager.

Don't be a bad boss. Let yourself have weekends and holidays off. Take sick days when you need them. When you're done with a school day, be done with it! Go do something totally different and fun that has no hidden educational purpose at all. Have a dance party. Watch a movie. Stare at a blank wall for a while, if that's what you need.

6. Educate Yourself

I am a self-proclaimed nerd. It was my downfall in junior high, when I had to suffer all the slings and spitballs of outrageous bullies. It is my great strength as the educator of my kids.

Whether you are a nerd or not, you can still continue to educate yourself as you educate your family. One of my favorite things to do as

I'm planning a year is to plan a few subjects for my own self-education. What do I want to learn about? What sounds fun or interesting?

When I first started homeschooling, my course of learning was about education and child-development. I checked out as many good books as I could find to help me know how to do this education thing. As the kids have gotten older, I've found topics from our history or science plans that I want to know more about. Often, as I'm searching for resources for their schooling, I come across a book about a topic that looks interesting. I once spent an entire fall reading half a dozen books for and against the theory of evolution so I would have a clearer understanding of that issue. This year, I'm trying to learn Korean and fighting to stay ahead of my kids in math. Since I expect them to completely master each of their grades in Khan Academy, I have made it my goal to master those levels before they do. Staying ahead helps me teach it to them when they get stuck, too, because I understand it for myself.

I don't do this because I feel like I should, but because I really enjoy it. However, I find that continuing my own learning does two things: it helps me keep my passion for teaching the children, and it earns me the children's respect as they see me continuing to learn new things just as they are. I'm modeling life-long learning for them.

You don't have to learn some topic you find utterly stifling. You might really enjoy being part of a drama club. You might want to learn to knit or quilt. You might enjoy reading biographies of famous musicians or politicians. You might want to learn bee-keeping or gardening. You can learn a musical instrument. Whatever it is, don't lose your curiosity. Keep learning about the things that interest you. That curiosity will carry over into your homeschooling life and help you be a better teacher of your children. It will also help you maintain a feeling of being an adult person with your own interests when you feel like you're drowning in crayons and construction paper.

As you can see, my main tips for the day-to-day work of homeschooling are to keep moving forward and to maintain your sanity. You might have different things that work for you to keep up your energy as you do the work. Keeping very visible values, as we discussed in the first section of this book, will go a long way toward keeping things good during your school days. I also find great relief in talking with my husband about my plans and how things are going. His ability to talk me through issues and offer encouragement is worth more than a hot cup of tea on a cold morning. Finding other homeschool parents to connect with can also be a great boost to your morale.

Reviewing and resetting

Preparing in advance for your weeks and managing your time well during the homeschool days will take you a great distance in your homeschool life, but sometimes you'll be going down a road you don't want to be on without realizing it. Sometimes, you won't be able to see the forest for the trees. For homeschoolers, it means you won't be able to see the learning through the stack of overdue library books and the mountain of laundry.

Two or three years ago, I was in the middle of a dreadful season of homeschooling when I felt like I wasn't accomplishing anything. I wanted someone to give me gold stars on a chart. I wanted a points system. I wanted some sort of boss to tell me I was doing okay, but there was no one else watching and even if there was, they couldn't see the things I could see. This is why I completely approve of those parents who choose to homeschool with a certified teacher overseeing their learning. Sometimes it helps to have someone else who can give you an idea of how you are doing. Homeschool communities are great for this kind of feedback, too, as long as they are not contributing to your feelings of inadequacy.

As I struggled through my feelings of discontent, I started making lists. I think I was trying to prove how little we were doing, but these lists proved just the opposite: we were doing many wonderful and amazing things. It's just that the majority of learning was happening outside of the scope of my chosen curriculum.

I started the habit of making a list every week of everything the kids had done or learned or talked about. As those lists filled up, I saw all the glorious work of a year building up in a physical mass. It was no wonder I was exhausted. I was emptying the contents of my brain into two unquenchable sponges from the moment I got up to the moment I passed out in my bed at night.

I've been doing weekly reviews ever since. They are for no one except myself. I file them away with the kids' records in case they're ever needed for something. Otherwise, they are simply a physical reminder to me of everything we do during the course of a homeschool week. They also help me stay on track with those yearly plans.

The review process lets me step back for a minute and get some fresh air. I get to see how things are going and decide if I need to make any changes. I often see that it's okay to take a break and have a play day here or there. It helps me stay sane during the crazy times. I highly recommend it as a good way to manage throughout your year.

I like to do a review once a week, usually on a Friday or Saturday as we finish the week of school. I will often write my review, and then go right into planning, and I get them both done at the same time. Reviewing once a week keeps all our activities fresh in my mind. I've tried doing monthly or quarterly reviews instead, but I can't remember what we did three weeks or a month ago. There's just too much to keep track of.

I don't like to do daily reviews for a similar reason. Writing everything down every day leaves a lot of gaps. There are subjects I don't cover every day. Some days are lighter than others. But as I write my reviews for a week's worth of school, I start seeing how things balance out. Instead of a lopsided day of just science and another day heavy on language arts, I see a fairly balanced week covering all the major subjects.

How you go about the review is up to you, but I recommend writing it down somewhere. Being able to look back on a stack of papers full of notes about what you did can really help you see the monumental task you're undertaking one day at a time.

If you want to do a weekly review to help you stay on track during your year, here are a few suggestions.

1. Check your plans.

When you sit down to review the week you just finished, it helps to start by looking at the plans you made for the week. Did you complete everything you hoped to complete? How did it go? Is there anything you missed that you want to cover next week? Is there anything you did that you wish you hadn't wasted time on?

I often go through my weekly plans and check off or draw a star by all the things we completed that week. Depending on what we did, I might make a small note next to books or videos whether they were favorites or duds. When I'm feeling very generous, I'll sit down and write Amazon reviews for some of them, too.

If there's anything we missed that I want to make sure we get to, I'll write a note about it on the next week's sheet, or I'll see where else we can fit it into future plans.

2. Write a subject review.

When you made your goals for the year, you included a number of subjects to cover. One of my favorite ways to monitor whether I'm actually meeting my goals is to keep a weekly review sheet. This is another way of seeing the forest without all those pesky trees getting in the way.

I make a grid on a sheet of paper, one large section for each of the major subjects my kids are studying. At the end of the week, for each child, I write down everything we did that would be included for each of those subjects. I think back to conversations we had, books we read, texts we studied, and games we played. What I usually discover, when I think we haven't done much of anything, is that we've covered a huge number of subjects and topics.

On September 11, we went to our weekly park day. As we drove by the government building, the kids noticed that all the flags were at half-mast and asked why. They'd heard about September 11 from history books before, but here was a chance to talk about it when there was a very visual reminder. We spent that entire car ride and the first several minutes at the park talking about what happened that day and how it changed things about our lives. Was that scheduled into the curriculum for the week? Nope. Did I write it on my review under history? You bet I did.

When I write my weeklies, I try to include everything. I don't just include whatever chosen curriculum I tortured everyone with. I also include how the kids care for their terrarium full of garden snails. I include the messages they write to their grandparents in Google Hangouts. I include their drawings and video game sketches and snippets of code they write. I include the hands-on games they play that act out all those concepts we study. I include the market they create to sell their handmade necklaces to the neighborhood kids. I include the video games they play. I include the movies they watch.

By the time I'm done looking back at the week, I'm almost always quite satisfied with how much real-life and book learning took place. Half of it might be unplanned discovery learning. That's okay with me. Without these weekly reviews, I might forget all of that. I might focus too much on the curriculum and forget how much real life is happening.

There are weeks when nothing happens, too. There are weeks that have a small note about completing math and a note about doing something in daily language. I used to freak out about these weeks and make all sorts of noise about how I was failing as a parent. I've learned to settle down since then. These are my bare minimums, remember? Those are enough. And when I get to the end of a year, and I have a stack of thirty-six full weeks written out, that one week is a tiny drop in a huge ocean of discoveries. There are other weeks where the chart is so full of notes I can't squeeze in one more book title. It all balances out.

This is a marathon, not a sprint. Writing out the weekly reviews helps me see that. It also helps me see how much we're doing, even when it doesn't feel like we're doing much.

If a weekly review feels like too much for you, try a monthly review instead. Any sort of time when you can look back on how your school year is going and think of ways to adjust is great.

3. What went well?

In terms of your homeschool life itself, what went well this week? What were those sparkling moments in the sea of chaos that made you think, "We're really doing something special here"?

I have been helping my daughter through each of her math questions daily. That means I usually sit by her while she does her Khan Academy, and I read the questions out loud. If it's a question about something obscure like gigabytes on a hard drive, I translate it into something she's interested in like ponies or unicorns. As she works on things like adding or subtracting over ten, I talk her through the process and ask her for different ideas about how to solve it.

A few weeks ago, as I sat down next to her to work on math with her, she told me, "I don't think I need you today, Mom. I can do this by myself." I couldn't decide how I felt about it. I had never been so proud for being stabbed in the heart. In reflection, that was one of the things that went well that week. I couldn't easily quantify it on a grades sheet. It's not like I could give her an A+ for independence. It was more like a guidepost that let me see progress was happening.

As you think over the week, try to remember good moments or interesting things that you and the kids did. Was there a way you changed your teaching for a subject that worked particularly well? Did you try to take more breaks or get better sleep? Did you make any small changes that made your days go better?

4. What could have gone better?

Notice the wording here. I didn't ask "What should have gone better?" Sometimes things happen during a homeschool week that are totally unpreventable. Someone gets sick and spends a night vomiting, throwing off the entire next day. Your toddler goes on a rampage when you aren't looking and empties a bag of flour on the dog. Sure, you might wish those things hadn't happened, but there's not much you could have done about it.

When I ask what could have gone better, I mean what things did you have control over that could have happened differently?

For me, these could haves usually refer to an attitude adjustment on my part. I could have been more patient. I could have taught that in a more interesting way instead of lecturing. I could have gone to bed earlier the night before so I wasn't a grouchy mess in the morning. I could have made sure to communicate better about what I expected the kids to work on. I could have spent more time on our creative writing assignment and less time stressing over spelling.

What things that you had power over could have gone better? Can you change those in the upcoming weeks?

5. Revise your plans.

The review is not just to help you see what you did, but also to help you see how to manage things better in the future. If you had too many things planned for this past week, you can take your review time to see how to manage those plans. Do you need to shift anything forward to future weeks? Are there topics that just need to be cut completely for the time being? Is there anything you would like to add?

As I reviewed my plans last year, I started to notice an interesting pattern. My daughter was not getting anything out of history. I would have these long drawn out discussions with my son about historical patterns and events, but the girl would be off playing somewhere during those times. She had completely disengaged.

As I noticed this in the weekly reviews, I started to think of ways to make history better for her. I asked my homeschool group for some suggestions, knowing that there are a lot of very creative moms in that group. They gave me dozens of wonderful ideas for ways to focus my daughter's attention, most notably the tips on focusing on fashion, food, and the role of women in those historical events. They also recommended I add more hands-on projects, which is exactly what I needed to do. My daughter has since become a great lover of history.

She even has her own Civil War play set, one of her favorites because she learned about the women who nursed the men back to health after battles.

As you review the week you just finished, see if there are any changes you can make to the way you do things. If you feel like you need to change something, but you're not sure what, talk it over with another homeschool friend or your homeschool community. They might have ideas to offer that you never thought of.

If you get off track

At some point in any given school year, especially if you've had any event that made you resort to your bare minimums for any amount of time, you might feel like you've gotten off track. What do you do if you're in the middle of a school year and you can't even figure out what week you're on?

When we made our sudden cross-country move last year, I had very little time or warning to manage everything. Last year was my spreadsheet year, when everything was laid out in such lovely color-coded plans that I could hardly even stand myself. Then, in a totally unplanned series of events, we were moving to a new state in the middle of winter. In less than six weeks, I had to pack up my house, find homes for my beloved pets, and find a new place to live.

By the time I unpacked in the new apartment and could get to the grocery store and home again without getting lost, I had no idea what week of the school year we should be on.

Sure, I had kept up with some of it. When I finally looked back and managed reviews, I saw that we had really only lost two weeks of school during that time. Since I had resorted to my bare minimum plans, the kids kept up with math, reading, and language. However, I had lost a significant portion of all the history, geography, foreign language, art, music, and science plans I had made. What to do?

If you're in a similar state for any reason, especially burn out, don't worry. There are a few things you can do to get back on track and finish out your school year.

1. Review your values.

Before you do anything else, take a minute to look at your values. Are they still the same? Did your non-schooling period alter your fundamental beliefs about education in any way? If your values have shifted, pick a new way to symbolize those values for yourself. If your values remain the same, review your favorite quote or phrases to help you remember why you're doing this.

Depending on your reasons for getting off track, a quick look at your values might revive your passion again. When I feel myself slipping and I talk to my husband about it, he will often be the one to point out my chosen values and tell me where I'm missing something. Sometimes, you just need someone to remind you about the things that are important to you.

2. Review the school you've done.

Unless you have completely tossed education out the window for several months, it's possible that you only lost a week or two in there. Go back and review. What subjects and topics did you cover during your off weeks that you can count toward schooling? Did you read something? Did you go to the store and figure out how much an item might cost with tax, or weigh oranges on a scale? Before you let yourself sink into despair, think of all the things you did get through during that time. Think of any opportunities you had that might be adding value to the lives of your children. If someone was sick and you were in and out of doctor's offices, that counts as a learning experience. It's not a pleasant learning experience, but it's still an experience.

Try to be kind to yourself here. It's easy for homeschool parents to add "feel guilt" to their ongoing list of things to do. If you are having trouble seeing what you've done, try to talk with a friend about it and ask them to help you review. Imagine you're the one helping your friend review. What would you say to him or her, without adding feelings of failure or guilt into the picture?

Once you've reviewed, try to figure out whether you need to add extra school weeks to your year or whether you can just jump back in with your previously scheduled calendar.

3. Reset the calendar.

Depending on how much you covered in your review, you might find that you need to add an extra week or two to finish out your school year in good conscience. You may have discovered that you stayed on track and aren't actually behind on the calendar. If you feel like you need to make some calendar adjustments, do that now. Figure out how many weeks are left in your school year. Set a new target end date if you need to.

When I was adjusting last year, I knew that I had lost two solid weeks of school when the kids had done nothing but watch Garfield cartoons while I packed and unpacked boxes. I found my school calendar in one of the boxes, and used it to count weeks again. Starting from the date I would start school again, I counted the number of weeks left to finish our school year on my originally planned end date. We had nine weeks left. I added two extra weeks to the end of the year to make up for what we had lost, which gave me eleven weeks to plan for. Sadly, we had only made it through week 20 before things went so crazy I couldn't keep up anymore. So there were at least five weeks of my plans that were completely lost, apart from our bare minimums.

4. Revise your goals.

Remember the goals section, where we talked about making things specific, measurable, achievable, reasonable, and time-bound? Well, you just took achievable and time-bound off the list. Again, don't feel guilt about this. Simply recognize that the goals you made before are null and void now. It's time to revise them.

Look at any subject specific goals now, and be realistic. Will you be able to finish the year in that curriculum by your new end date? How much will you have to adjust in order to make it? Do you just need to add an extra page or two a week, or is it such a significant change that it's no longer possible?

For any subject that didn't require a finished textbook, where will you start up again? If it's a subject that requires a level of proficiency, like a language or a mastery-based program, do you need to back up and review? Where should you start again?

5. Cut unnecessary subjects or topics.

If you're just waking up from a difficult period of time, it might be necessary to cut way back on your schooling for the rest of the year or for several weeks. If this is the case, look through those daily lists of subjects and see what you can cut out entirely. When I finished out last year, I let my Latin and music appreciation plans go, and I cut art back to once every two weeks. I felt sad about it, because those were some of my favorite extras, but it was too much. Besides, we were having all sorts of new learning experiences as we got to know the people and locations in our new town.

A thing that interrupts your school year won't always be a fun new experience. Sometimes it will be a death in the family or a serious illness or emergency. Remember that it takes a lot of time and energy to recover from these types of things, and you will need to grieve in many cases. Give yourself the space to do that.

6. Re-cut your curriculum.

This is the point at which the modular weekly system is wonderfully flexible. Since I had weekly topics and units for science and history all planned out, I was able to go through my plans and pick out the eleven most important things I wanted to study to finish out the year. Yes, that meant I lost several weeks of fantastic plans. I had to decide which things were more important and which could be skimmed over.

For other subjects, this means deciding whether you will skip or skim certain parts in order to complete it on time.

I don't recommend trying to cram everything in if you've lost several weeks of school. You might be tempted to just do more in every single subject to finish the year. Please don't do it. If you're just coming out of a season of illness or burnout, you might need to plan even less than before as you recover. This is okay. This is what those bare minimums are for. Be realistic as you look at how to finish your year.

7. Write new plans.

One sure way to make yourself feel guilty for the rest of the school year is to keep using the same plans you had before, while trying to remember that you cut something here and didn't do something there. Don't torture yourself. Make a fresh set of plans to finish out your school year.

In my case, this was eleven weeks of plans. Now, building an entire school year from scratch can be a time-consuming process, as you have now experienced. But making a quilt out of school plans that got eaten by moths is not nearly as difficult. You just cut something here, add something there, stitch it together, and call it good.

I made eleven new weekly sheets, wrote in my topics, double-checked that the new library had the books I needed, found other books if not, and then went with it. This reset, from the first step to the final product, took me about half a day. I was amazed at how easy it was. Because my plans were solid before the school year started, reorganizing them was not a difficult process.

Finding a homeschool community

I'd like to make a note here about the importance of good homeschool communities.

I recently moved from Washington State to Southern California. A few things here are very different. For instance, there is a fiery light that burns down from the sky here in California, and there are no rainclouds to protect us from its wrath. The trees here are tall and scraggly, more like Dr. Seuss creations than the solid presence of the fir trees in Washington. The traffic is very different, too. Washington traffic and California traffic are both dreadful, but for opposite reasons. Washington drivers are too nice and will stop in the middle of the freeway to let someone get on at 25 miles per hour. California drivers are trained in offensive driving and you have to stay sharp if you don't want to get run over.

For all the differences, there is one thing that is exactly the same. The homeschool groups are filled with dozens of different families all using different methods and curricula.

There is the theater mom, whose kids are all creative and on the go from dawn until dusk. There is the unschooling mom whose kid has taken an interest in getting his Linux certification and is devouring every resource on the subject. There is the Classical Conversations mom whose entire family, including the two-year old, has memorized the history timeline and thinks it's fun to diagram sentences. There is the unit studies mom who is currently teaching about France and can spout off a thousand fun facts about the country, including the mathematics involved in the architecture of the Eiffel Tower.

In my five years in homeschool co-ops and support groups, I can tell you one thing: there's something for everyone.

Homeschool groups get a bad reputation sometimes. It's hard for many parents to find the group that is the right fit. Homeschoolers who don't subscribe to a particular religion often feel alienated by the groups that do, and vice versa. A group might exist that is serving the needs of a couple of its core members, but is failing to help others who need something entirely different. Personalities clash. In my experience, people who choose to homeschool are often a fairly confident and independent bunch anyway, and it's easy for two people to disagree on major issues. I see a lot of homeschool bloggers railing against the co-op and saying they will never join a homeschool group because they've had bad experiences.

It doesn't have to be this way. In homeschool communities that function well, parents can offer each other many resources and new opportunities that no one could have on their own. I've always loved the great variety of skills and styles I find in my homeschool groups. If

I have trouble finding resources for a particular subject, I can ask for help from my homeschool group. There is almost always someone in there who is especially interested in the subject I'm asking about. There is usually someone who is fantastic with math, or someone who geeks out about literature. I have friends who text me grammar questions or math questions, and in return, I beg for creative resources for history. We all can help each other.

When I talk about homeschool communities, I don't mean that you should join an organized co-op that teaches a class on biology every Thursday at 10 a.m. What I mean is that being connected to other homeschoolers in some way is beneficial, not just for you and your kids, but for those other homeschool families, too.

Homeschool communities can take a lot of different forms. Some groups join up specifically to have co-op classes. Other groups only have park days and social events. Other groups share resources with each other and have planning sessions. Others are just online groups that talk about various aspects of local homeschooling. These groups can be difficult to find and can sometimes be difficult to get involved with, but once you are part of one of these groups, the benefits can be significant. Depending on your particular needs and the needs of your family, you can decide how much you want to participate.

If you aren't part of your local homeschooling community, I highly recommend getting involved. If there is not a group in your area, consider forming your own. You don't have to teach classes. You could form a group devoted to playdates, online encouragement, or resource sharing. Being around other people who are homeschooling can be a very encouraging thing. Rather than feeling odd and isolated, you might discover that what you are going through is a very normal experience for the majority of people devoted to home education.

Final Notes

Process review

This book has covered a lot of tough territory. You made it through all the exercises and now have the plans for an entire year of schooling. Congratulations! I hope you have a fantastic year. I hope that all the work on finding your values and setting realistic goals will help you as you work through educating your children at home.

If all the exercises and steps seemed like too much for you, that's okay, too. The true goal of this book is to help you set up your homeschool year in a way that makes sense for you and your family. It originally started as a way to explain to my friends how I planned my own curriculum every year, and it grew into the monster you're reading. I realized that I couldn't talk about building my own curriculum without talking about all those other things that go into my yearly planning.

Here's the entire process at a glance.

Find Your Values.

It will be extremely difficult to do well in home education if you don't know what is important to you about it. It can also be hard to find homeschool communities that share your values if you don't know what they are or what you are looking for. Spend some time figuring out what's most important to you, and things will begin to fall into place.

Discover Your Ideal Methods.

You can wade into the ocean of available curricula without any idea of what you want, or you can spend some time familiarizing yourself with the various types of education that are already out there. Depending on your teaching style, the learning style of your children, and the evaluation styles that work best for you, some curricula will work better for you than others.

Look at the Big Picture.

You're not just homeschooling a third grader right now. You're doing the difficult work of preparing a child to become an adult. Spend some time thinking about what kind of adult you hope to raise. Visualizing future possibilities can help you decide how to manage the present.

Set SMART Goals.

It's always nice to set goals, but it's disappointing when you can't actually accomplish them. The secret to making goals that will work is to make them specific, measurable, achievable, realistic, and time-bound. As you work through your plans, ask yourself if your goals fit those specifications. Set yourself up to succeed by setting good goals.

Decide what subjects you'll teach each week.

Spread them out into the days of the week. Now take a look at how much time all of that will take and decide whether it's going to work for you. Revise as necessary.

Set Bare Minimums.

If everything else goes crazy, what school subjects or requirements will still get you through it? What are the things you think are absolutely necessary to cover during a school day or week? Decide on these now. Write them down somewhere in your homeschool planner or notebook, so you can look at them when you need them.

Choose Your Curricula.

Based on your values, methods, and goals, what programs will work best to help you teach your chosen subjects this year? If you need help finding curricula, ask a local group of homeschoolers or search online. There might be curriculum counselors in your area who specialize in helping homeschoolers find curricula for their particular needs. Decide what you'll be using.

Plan Your Own Curricula.

If you know what you want, but can't find it to purchase, create your own curricula for your subjects for the year. This is a time-consuming task, but not particularly difficult. Choose a good spine or list of topics, and then find resources to help you teach them.

Make Yearly and Monthly Overviews.

Looking over all the events that will happen during your school year can help significantly as you plan for your school days. Make sure you know where all your recurring events are going to fall during your year. Mark out your first and last days of school.

Set Up Weekly Plans.

Divide your school year into a number of weeks. This will make it easier to break down your curriculum and decide how much you need to complete each week. Find out if you need to divide your curriculum by page numbers, unit studies, or practice times. For any unit-based topics, add them individually to your weekly plans so you can see at a glance every major topic you'll study each week.

Finalize.

Make final copies and backups of any of your plans. File them all together in a place where you can easily get to them during your school year.

Prepare, Present, and Review.

As you go through your school year, remember to look ahead at the coming weeks so you can prepare. Make habits out of your daily requirements so you can keep things running smoothly. Review often and revise your plans as necessary. If you get off track, review what you've done and rebuild your plans so you can finish out your year.

Recommended resources

For a list of recommended resources, printables, and other helpful information, please visit

www.blueprinthomeschooling.com

Contact information

A full year of homeschooling is an arduous task, whether you plan for it or not. I have great respect for all the parents who undertake it each and every year. I hope that reading this book has encouraged you and given you some ideas for making your year easier and more manageable.

If you have any questions about the process, or would like to share how this book has helped you, I would love to hear from you! Feel free to contact me at amy@blueprinthomeschooling.com.

Acknowledgments

I always thought writing a book was a secret and solitary achievement—a thing that you do by yourself in a quiet room when no one is looking. Boy, was I wrong. I am eternally grateful to the many people who have supported and encouraged me through the two-year long process of writing, editing, and publishing *Blueprint Homeschooling*.

I owe the idea itself to the families in the Lewis County Elementary Homeschool Co-op, who asked for help and advice as they started homeschooling and then encouraged me to write a book about my ideas. I am eternally grateful to Sarah Gallagher, whose consistent nagging forced me to keep working when I wanted to quit. Christy Johnson, Angela Wilcox, Janessa Anzelini, Stella Eiswald, and many others will see themselves in my stories. Thank you for being a part of my life.

My move to California introduced me to the Arroyo Verde Explorers, the best group of homeschoolers in Southern California. I feel blessed to be part of such a welcoming group. Holly, Nichole, Gabi, Michelle, Crystal, Bruce, and anyone else who listened to me rattle on about this and made the mistake of telling me it was a good idea—thank you.

It's still hard for me to believe that I was able to get Karen Conlin from Grammargeddon as my editor, but I'm so glad she agreed to work with me! She cleaned up my words and made them shine, and for that, I am incredibly grateful.

I never would have called myself a writer without meeting my tribe: Amy Ryding, Liz Kellebrew, Larry Roth, and Holly St. Clair. I'm thankful we're on this journey together. My writing has only improved since meeting the generous writers in the Writers' Discussion Group and the Pixel-Stained Writers community on Google+. It would take pages to list everyone, but I'm especially thankful to John Ward, Nathan Lowell, and Lisa Cohen, who made me believe I was up to the challenge. The Warren, the Shively, my arch-nemesis Rachel Desilets, Hobgoblin Greg, Jon Stone, Maya, Marti, and Masha have all kept me going when things were tough. Thank you all.

My parents always told me I could be whatever I wanted to be and meant it, and I'm thankful for their unconditional love and encouragement. I also have some of the most awesome kids in the world. I'm not sure I could do it without their constant cheerleading and ideas.

And last, but not least, I am incredibly thankful for my husband and best friend forever, Dave. He makes me laugh. I can't think of anything in life worth more than that.